The Transcenda Teen:
A 21st Century Guide to Emotional Enlightenment

Christy Engle

Transcend: To go beyond the limits of what was previously thought possible

What is Transcendentalism?

Transcendentalism was an American intellectual, spiritual, and philosophical movement which took place between the 1820's and 1830's. It emphasized the ideas of **individuality, self-reliance, nature, and independence.** Ralph Waldo Emerson and Henry David Thoreau were Transcendentalism's founding fathers. Throughout their years on this planet, both men left a legacy of writings which would have the transformative power to teach future generations important ideals needed for emotional enlightenment. These tools are ours for the taking. Let's utilize them.

What inspired the writing of this book?

Tough Times   Teens   Teaching   Transcendentalism

For 23 years now, I have been teaching Transcendentalism in my American Literature courses. Thankfully, the majority of my students (some of whom are very troubled) have gravitated toward, and connected with, Emerson and Thoreau's ideals. Last spring, it occurred to me that these men's 19th Century quotes could positively shape the mindsets of 21st Century teens, and so the book was conceived. These principles have the potential to change people's lives and their perspectives on it. I hope they do.

How **YOU** Will Use This Book:

This manual is designed for students to explore quotes left behind by two of the most enlightened thinkers of all time- Ralph Waldo Emerson and Henry David Thoreau. No doubt about it- these men were geniuses! They captured and shared the meaning of life, love and happiness almost 200 years ago, and yet they are grossly under-celebrated! Not anymore! Here, in this book, The Transcendental Teen: A 21st Century Guide to Emotional Enlightenment, we will honor and engage their ideas, and perhaps allow ourselves to adopt their inspirational suggestions, as a part of our own modern-day lives. By considering the quotes and passages presented, and by reflecting personally through writing, we, too, can become Transcendental thinkers, artists, writers, speakers, and philosophers. We **can** heal ourselves- One. Page. At. A. Time.

Throughout the book, I will pre-label each man's quote as follows:

RWE=RALPH WALDO EMERSON **HDT**=HENRY DAVID THOREAU

This way, you will know who wrote what!

The following is an example of how the book will manipulated:

A main topic will be listed, under which I will cite an "RWE" or "HDT" quote/s associated with it. Next, I will offer a modern-day interpretation of it, and then I will pose a question or topic for you to explore via personal written response.

See below:

RWE: "In every society, some men are born to rule, and some to advise."

We are not all here to command others; some of us merely act as guides. People have a tendency to lean towards certain leadership styles. One leads with ***directives*** and the other with ***direction***. Which style best suits how you would elect to lead?

WERE YOU BORN TO RULE OR ADVISE? WHY?

Personally, I feel I was born to advise. I have known, since being an adolescent myself, that I was destined to teach teens, and have been doing so for the past 23 years. From the onset, I felt no inclination to control my students. I treat all people as my equal, and try to lead others in a positive direction. I do not feel "ruling," of any sort, suits my leadership style. It goes counter to my personality. After all, if we control all of the choices for the people we are supposed to guide, how will they ever learn?

Okay, that's my answer. Now it's your turn.

Shall we begin?

Like seriously, when would NOW be a good time to start?

Individuality

RWE: "To be yourself in a world that is constantly trying to make you something else is the greatest accomplishment."

Some of my favorite students are those who devote their lives entirely to being themselves. No matter what, they maintain their way of dress, thinking, and behavior. Although it seems "alternative," it is what is what is best for the development of **_their_** own soul. These troopers of truth add so much vibrancy and intellect to the class. Their ideas challenge the unimaginative mainstream, and make orthodox others question themselves as thinkers and believers. Ironically, these evolved beings are often the most bullied. It is almost as though people see them as a threat for having succeeded in being authentic to themselves - something the ordinary population does not know how to do. Trust me, if you can continue to devote yourself to YOU, I promise that life will deliver far more successes and happiness than any conventional way of doing things ever will. Stay strong, and embrace yourself (literally and figuratively)! You'll be glad you did! How are you an individual? What sets you apart from the rest? How can this be deemed a good thing?

HOW I AM DIFFERENT AND WHY IT IS GOOD:

_____
_____
_____
_____
_____
_____
_____

Be You. Shame on this world for not letting you feel comfortable enough to do so. This society has been trying to shape you into something unnatural- a mirror's image of itself, and people who comply with its desire are sure to fail. If you can maintain the YOU that is YOU, you have already accomplished one of life's greatest feats! Who do you want to be? Why?

I WANT TO BE:

_____
_____
_____
_____

BECAUSE:

_____
_____
_____
_____

RWE: "Who you are speaks so loudly, I cannot hear what you are saying."

When you are truly being the influential you, it should ooze out of your being so obnoxiously, that people MUST take notice! I'm not talking about being a loudmouth a-hole. I am talking about letting your goodness be felt and understood by all who enter the room you inhabit! Your presence shouldn't be heard, it should be felt! You are energy. Let yourself be a battery of boldness. If you are committed to being yourself (which I hope you are), then PLEASE do so as overtly and loudly as you can. Let the YOU that is YOU be heard from all of the rooftops of the world! Let no one NOT sense your beauteous being! When you walk into a room, what energy do you emit? How do people react to your presence?

OTHERS' REACTION TO MY ENTRY INTO A ROOM:

_____
_____
_____
_____
_____
_____
_____

I MUST SAY THAT THIS IS A GOOD OR BAD THING, AND HERE IS WHAT I NEED TO DO TO WORK ON OR ENHANCE IT:

_____
_____
_____
_____
_____
_____
_____

RWE: "The secret of ugliness consists not in irregularity, but in being uninteresting."

People will often find others attractive when the stand for something- an ideal, a principle, a passion. If you go through your life banking on a blank slate bringing you a life, a love, or an ounce of happiness, think again. Nobody will want to date you or befriend you. Simply put: without interests, you are NOT interesting! Get out of that imprisoning bed, and start getting positively passionate about something! What are some of your current interests?

MY CURRENT INTERESTS INCLUDE:

_____
_____
_____
_____
_____
_____

HOW MIGHT YOUR INTERESTS ATTRACT OTHER PEOPLE TO YOU?

_____
_____
_____

RWE: "To be great is to be misunderstood."

If you are not well-understood; be grateful. Perhaps you are doing something right. Those who are NOT "gotten" by others are often deemed the most innovative thinkers and creators of their time. Insert great thinkers here: Joan of Arc, Martin Luther King, Jr., Buddha, Pythagoras, Christy Engle (had to include myself), Einstein, Ben Franklin, Thomas Edison, and Eleanor Roosevelt. Whom do you know who is greatly misunderstood by the majority, and what have they taught you that the others "mainstreamers" have not?

MISUNDERSTOOD PEOPLE I'VE KNOWN AND WHAT THEY HAVE TAUGHT ME:

_____
_____
_____
_____
_____
_____
_____

IN WHAT WAYS HAVE YOU BEEN MISUNDERSTOOD? WHY DO YOU THINK OTHERS HAVE NOT SEEN AND ACCEPTED THE REAL YOU?

_____
_____
_____
_____
_____
_____
_____

HDT: "If a man does not keep pace with his companions, perhaps it is because he hears a different drummer. Let him step to the music which he hears- however measured or far away."

Not everyone is going to think or act like you, and that, My Friends, is a damn good thing! If you see someone who acts differently or dresses in a unique manner, you should be celebrating them- not crucifying them! We need for people to step out in distinct ways. It makes the world so much more of an interesting place! Some people's tempo is slow and steady, while others' beats are fast and furious. Let's allow each other to hear and step to a flow that is entirely our own. What is your rhythm? How does it work for you?

MY RHYTHM AND WHAT IT DOES FOR ME:

_____
_____
_____
_____
_____

HDT: "There will never be a really free and enlightened State until the State comes to recognize the individual as a higher and independent power, from which all of its own power and authority are derived, and treats him accordingly."

This world has become a wrathful wreck, and we cannot free ourselves from its torturous grip, until we begin to genuinely permit **all** people to be their own authentic selves. Our governing bodies (as well as the common man) have got to start recognizing that all of the diversity on this populated planet is a bountiful blessing. We have so much to share with one another if, and only if, we begin to grant our citizens permission to be themselves. If this happens, people will begin to feel unburdened. They will become productive members of our society. They will desire **no** harm to others. An atmosphere of unity and enlightenment will be created naturally. Go ahead, visualize a place where people are allowed to be them SELVES? If permitted, who would you become? What might happen?

WHO I WOULD BECOME AND WHAT MIGHT HAPPEN?

_____
_____
_____
_____
_____
_____

Wake Up

HDT: "We must learn to reawaken and keep ourselves awake, not by mechanical aid, but by an infinite expectation of the dawn."

We need to wake up for the sake of living, and not just because our cell phone's alarm clock alerts us to do so. We are motivated by technology, when we should be driven by life. Let us look forward to each new day with an anticipation of something natural and great- not another day of digitalization. We are living, breathing beings, and so we need to get out and actually inhale the fresh air that surrounds us. This isolative age of love for one's touchscreen has got to diminish. People, we are losing sight of why were are here; it is to connect, and yet we are not connected. We may talk to each other through our phones or computers, but nothing can compete with human-to-human proximity. We need each other, and we need to stay alert, each day, in order to truly be together. Let's make a concerted effort to try- to try to remove ourselves from the "mechanical aids," and reawaken to the beauty that is life. The "infinite dawn" is ours to seize.

BESIDES AN ALARM CLOCK, WHAT REALLY WAKES YOU UP IN YOUR LIFE?

_____
_____
_____
_____
_____
_____

WITH WHOM DO YOU NEED TO RE-ESTABLISH A RELATIONSHIP THAT HAS BEEN LOST? WHY?

_____
_____
_____
_____
_____
_____

Overcoming Obstacles

RWE: "Bad times have a scientific value. These are occasions a good learner would not miss."

There is so much of a gift wrapped up in every barrier you face. Please don't miss the opportunity to unwrap yours. I was a troubled teen. I had divorced parents, an alcoholic dad, deplorable money problems, and yes, crappy grades. I was being bullied at school, and did not get along with my mom. I left home at 15, and lived with my aunt and uncle for a year. Every night, I cried myself to sleep. I could not figure out why my life was always in shambles. I wondered why I had so many issues, and it seemed like everyone else's lives were marvelously magnificent. One night I prayed. I had never really prayed much before that, but this night was different. I literally got on my hands and knees and began to beg for help. The next day, things began to change. I felt hope creeping into me. I decided that my life could change, and it was entirely up to me. I realized that perhaps my obstacles were meant to teach me something useful, and by golly, they did! Because of my struggles, I became a magnificent mother and teacher. I understood people better than most others. I could relate to their problems, and help them find viable solutions. Through my pain, I unwrapped my gifts, and am now able to share them with you and countless others. You see, my friends, every time you curse your negative circumstances, you miss a chance for growth. Embrace these difficulties, as they are the building blocks for your future life- a life you will use to help others, who, too, may struggle to understand. What obstacles do you currently face, and how might they someday help others?

MY OBSTACLES AND HOW THEY MIGHT HELP OTHERS:

_____
_____
_____
_____
_____
_____

RWE: "The greatest glory in living lies not in never falling, but in rising every time we fall."

You will grow significantly, if you continue to pick yourself up after you are knocked down. Many teens feel that when one really awful thing happens to them, they cannot get back up. This defeatist mindset has got to change. It is in the "getting up" that the most growth is achieved. Quit protecting yourself from making mistakes, experiencing failures, and facing your fears. These are the ruthless roots of what makes us strong. I have watched countless students come through my doors who have endured crippling (literally and figuratively) events that they could have clung to as debilitating moments, but instead, they elected to pull themselves up by the bootstraps, and push forward. Dysfunctional parents, deaths of family members, horrible teachers, problems with bullies, physical ailments and deformities, and most of them chose- AND it IS a choice- NOT to allow these obstacles interfere with their success. So can you. What obstacles have knocked you on your rear end? How did you get back up? If you did not rise up, how can you?

OBSTACLES I FACED AND HOW I PICKED MY SORRY BUTT UP:

_____
_____
_____
_____
_____

RWE: "As long as man stands in his own way, everything seems to be in his way."

Get out of the way of yourself, and the others you blame will disappear. Wow! It is so easy for us to prevent ourselves from success, but yet we blame every bit of our failure on everyone else- teachers, parents, society, classmates, races, religions, etc. What a joke! Whom can we blame for the lack of advancement in our lives? You guessed it- ourselves. We need to take ownership. We can only accuse our one-and-only self-indulgent, lazy, excuse-making selves! Do yourself a favor; get out of your own frickin' way. Make room for the new triumphant you! What are you doing to get in your own way right now? Whom or what do you blame?

I GET IN MY OWN WAY BY:

_____
_____
_____
_____
_____
_____

I NEED TO STOP BLAMING: _____

BECAUSE:

_____
_____
_____
_____
_____
_____

Life

RWE: "Life is a succession of lessons which must be lived to be understood."

A lot of times my own children (both teens) or students will ask me what the purpose of life is. Now, this is a pretty loaded and tough question to answer, but usually my response is something like this, "Life is like school. You are here to learn as many lessons as you can. Some lessons you will enjoy learning. Others, you will hate, but in the end, the more lessons you learn, the easier your life will become." The problem is, most people do not learn their lessons (just like in school), and they have to keep repeating classes or tests until the material is understood. It behooves you (which means it is a damn good idea) to absorb as many experiences as you possibly can, so that you can learn to grow and change according to the master plan- which, by the way, was designed by YOU! What life lessons have you lived and learned? What have they taught you? What life lessons have you not yet mastered? Why is it important for you to learn these?

LIFE LESSONS I HAVE LEARNED:

_____
_____
_____
_____
_____
_____
_____

THESE LESSONS HAVE TAUGHT ME:

_____
_____
_____
_____
_____
_____
_____

LIFE LESSONS I HAVE NOT YET MASTERED:

_____
_____
_____
_____
_____
_____
_____

I NEED TO MASTER THESE, BECAUSE IF I DO NOT:

_____
_____
_____
_____
_____
_____
_____

RWE: "We are always getting ready to live but never living."

We prepare for a lot, but we do not live. Why do we spend so much time making arrangements to live, instead of just getting out there and doing it- living it? It is difficult to plan and plot out every step we will take. It does not have to be that contrived. We can simply make immediate decisions to live an interesting life, and execute them. Living *is* now. It is spontaneous. It is fun. It is not calculated.

I CAN BEGIN LIVING NOW BY:

_____
_____
_____
_____
_____
_____

RWE: "Life is our dictionary."

You want a definition of living? Live it! Every experience we have is teaching us something super valuable. It might be something good, or it might be something bad, but it *is* teaching you, and you can only define it on your own terms- based on your perceptions of the experiences **you** have. Therefore, "Life is our dictionary." What has life taught you lately? What definition do you give your life?

LIFE HAS SO FAR TAUGHT ME:

_____
_____
_____
_____
_____
_____

I WOULD DEFINE MY LIFE AS:

_____
_____
_____
_____
_____
_____

It's "Your" Fault

RWE: "Every man in his lifetime needs to thank his faults."

We all have issues. None of us is perfect, but this can be deemed a good thing. Our faults remind us of the work we still need accomplish regarding the development of ourselves. When we are procrastinators, we need to own up to it. When we are rude, we need to own up to it.

When we are inactive, we need to own up to it. When we eat gluttonously, we need to own up to it. This acknowledgment of our flaws will only help us to grow into more evolved versions of ourselves. It is only when we are in denial or rejection of these issues, that we stymy our growth.

WHAT ARE YOUR FAULTS, AND HOW CAN YOU WORK ON THEM?

_____
_____
_____
_____
_____
_____

Appearances

RWE: "People that seem so glorious are all show; underneath they are all like everyone else.

We look at famous actors, professional athletes, renowned singers, and prize-winning writers, and we think that they are untouchables. We need to see that this is oftentimes just an illusion. What these individuals wear, the cars they drive, homes they occupy, and the faces they sport are not always the real deal. These folks are humans- like us, and although they possess a talent or beauty unbeknownst to us, they are no more magnificent than we. The person in whom we should invest the most stock is ourselves. It is the inner appearance that matters most. What does **that** look like? What is inside of people is what needs to be seen, for it is NOT illusory. It speaks the truth.

WHAT IS YOUR INSIDE APPEARANCE?

_____
_____
_____
_____
_____
_____

IS IT GOOD OR BAD, AND HOW CAN YOU ENHANCE OR ELIMINATE THIS PERCEPTION?

_____
_____
_____
_____
_____
_____

HDT: It is an interesting question how far men would retain their relative rank if they were divested of their clothes."

Simply put, without a flashy wardrobe, all men stack up the same. We pay too much attention to how important a person is based on his/her attire, and this is so wrong. We should be placing emphasis upon people's character and contributions- not their designer label jeans, expensive yoga pants or imported boots. We are all equal, Kids, and to think that we are less because we cannot afford to keep up with all of the fancy stitches is pure lunacy! No costume covering can define us or make us less or more worthy. We are equals, because we are the same underneath it all- we are HUMAN! The sooner we get that through our thick skulls, the sooner we can evolve as a collective body of beings.

ASIDE FROM THE OBVIOUS (PEOPLE WOULD ALL BE NAKED), WHAT MIGHT THE WORLD BE LIKE IF CLOTHES WERE NEVER INVENTED? WHAT MIGHT BE OUR MAIN FOCUS? WOULD THE WORLD BE BETTER OR WORSE? HOW?

_____
_____
_____
_____
_____
_____
_____

Courage

RWE: "Every man has his own courage, and is betrayed because he seeks in himself, the courage of other persons."

We live vicariously through the bravery and victories of others. Instead, we need to capture our own courage, and realize its potential. Think about how much time we spend watching NFL games, infomercials about weight loss success, and people truly making a difference. We sit passively- admiring others' heroic efforts to do difficult tasks, but we never stop to realize that we, too, are capable of great feats. When are we going to start to pursue our own talents and purposes for being here? What are you afraid to do, but could easily try today?

THINGS I AM AFRAID TO DO, BUT AM WILLING TO TRY TODAY:

_____
_____
_____
_____
_____
_____

Enthusiasm

HDT: "None are so old as those who have outlived enthusiasm."

If you are not enthusiastic, you may as well be OLD as hell. A lot of people are living a mediocre existence. They do not inject enthusiasm in their life. This mundane attitude gets them nowhere. The greatest thinkers, writers, speakers, and inventors had one thing in common: they were enthusiastic! They got excited about their ideas, and that zest for what was like a positive contagion to others. What are you enthusiastic about, and what do you need to get enthusiastic about? How can you do this? What might happen if you do?

I AM ENTHUSIASTIC ABOUT_____.

I NEED TO GET ENTHUSIASTIC ABOUT_____. I CAN DO

THIS BY: _____.

IF I DO THIS, PERHAPS:

_____
_____
_____
_____
_____
_____

WILL HAPPEN.

RWE: "Nothing great was ever achieved without enthusiasm."

This is a truism. If you do not get excited about something, how can anyone else? Most of the world's most notable thinkers have simply banked (literally and figuratively) on this quote, and it is how they accomplished greatness. Think about some of your lame frickin' teachers who come to class each day- miserable and not excited about the content they teach. They speak in a monotone manner, use no gestures of excitement, and act as though their being there is just a paycheck-receiving opportunity. Their enthusiasm for teaching is as about contagious as a germ's pouncing on an anti-bacterial soap and surviving. Your desire to attend their class is about as tempting as the majority of mankind going on a strict vegan diet. FOR A LIFETIME. People, PLEASE get enthusiastic about life. It is such an absolute blessing. Think about how many times negative, nasty people have sucked the crap out of a generally great moment. Is this how you wish to be deemed- a fecal matter-sucking, monumental moment-stealer? Inject excitement. It is the maker of greatness. When are times people stole a potentially good moment from you with their lack of enthusiasm? What were you thinking or wishing?

PEOPLE WHO SUCKED THE GOOD MOMENT AWAY AND WHAT IT DID TO ME:

_____
_____
_____
_____
_____
_____

OH, HOW I THOUGHT or WISHED I HAD:

_____
_____
_____
_____
_____
_____

Fear

RWE: "Always do what you are afraid to do."

Not rocket science, People. Just grow a pair (of wings, Silly!). Do what you thought you could not. Be fearless in the face of adversity. I once auditioned for a movie. I had never acted in my life before, but something told me to go for it. I did. I knew the internal push to do so was super strong, and I could not contain the desire to follow a new passion of mine. I abandoned all of my fears, and just went for it. After 3 difficult improvisational meetings with the producer and a casting agent, I astounded my family, friends, and students by landing the lead role in one of today's most compelling movies about bullying- "A Girl Like Her." I did what I (in the past) thought was impossible, and I persevered! After that feat, I felt I could do anything my heart desired. What are you afraid to do or try? What or who is stopping you? How can you stop "it?"

THINGS I AM AFRAID TO TRY AND WHAT I WILL DO TO THAT OR THOSE WHO TRY TO STOP ME:

_____
_____
_____
_____
_____
_____
_____

RWE: "He who is not every day conquering some fear has not learned the secret of life."

Throughout my life, I have been somewhat fearless- bungee jumping, parasailing, and riding formidable rollercoasters, but the scariest thing I ever did was divorce my ex-husband. I knew once I did it, it would rape me financially, rob my kids emotionally, and change my life drastically, but I KNEW I had to do it to amass tranquility. I did it. It was ten years ago, and it is one of the most rewarding decisions I have made to date. At first, I was afraid to let go of the nightmare. Why? Was I a glutton for punishment? Hells no! I eventually I mustered up the courage to file the delicious divorce papers. I had a fantastic flavor of freedom and happiness I had never tasted before. Someone had to be brave. That someone was me. What are times you overcame your fears? What did that do for you emotionally?

TIMES I OVERCAME MY FEARS AND WHAT IT DID FOR ME:

_____
_____
_____
_____
_____
_____

RWE: "Fear defeats more people than any other one thing in the world."

Why do so many of us subscribe to fear? It is detrimental in so many ways. It destroys aptitude, relationships, fun, success and a whole slew of other otherwise great opportunities for growth. We must stop allowing fear to wrap its ugly arms around us- putting a chokehold on any chance we have of living the life we were meant to pursue. Think about some ways in which fear has destroyed or paralyzed you, and list them below. Next, come up with a few ways that you can combat those fears in the future.

FEARS THAT F-ED ME UP AND WAYS I CAN BEAT THEM AWAY WITH A SILLY STICK:
_____
_____
_____
_____
_____
_____

Friendship

RWE: "The only way to have a friend is to be one.

Pretty self-explanatory. If you want more friends, you better be one yourself. This is so simple, but very few people can understand it. If you want more people to hang out with, be nice! I teach a teenage boy who constantly complains about not having many friends. Every night he goes to his room and plays video games. He does not join any clubs at school, never asks other kids to hang out, and is generally (on the daily) pissed off at his schoolmates who "never include him" for parties and sporting events. I have told him several times, that perhaps he should initiate the invitations - to ask people to go out and mingle, but he cannot, does not, and will not. Can you say, "stubborn?" He sees no correlation between his anti-social antics, and the subsequent apathy on the part of the others to invite him. People, to be a friend, you have to be there for others. If they do not see you are interested in them, they will not be interested in you! DUH! How can you be a friend today? What might happen if you decided to do so?

WAYS I CAN BE NICE AND INCLUDE OTHERS AND WHAT MIGHT HAPPEN AS A RESULT:
_____
_____
_____
_____
_____
_____

We want so badly to blame society for all of our rejection, when we actually reject "it" as well. Ironic, don't you think? When can we stop blaming others for their exclusion of us, when in reality, with our negative thoughts and expectations, we should take total responsibility for having excluded ourselves? When have you complained about not getting invited to do something with others? What might you have contributed to make the others not invite you?

THE TIME I DIDN'T GET INVITED AND HOW I CAUSED IT:
_____
_____
_____

_____
_____
_____

HDT: "The most I can do for my friend is simply be his friend."

Friends are such an integral part of our lives. Just as we need them; they need us. Often our friends will desperately seek our being there for them. This is exactly what we need to do. We do not necessarily need to give our unsolicited advice about their every move or choice. Instead, we should just remain present in their lives, to let them know we care, and can help- if needed. We should have our friends' backs. We should not betray them with deceit, lies, and manipulation. Our friends deserve for us to be the best version of ourselves by loving them, accepting them, forgiving them, and supporting them in every capacity. You know these friends. You have hopefully had or have them. Who were/are they, and how were they a friend to you?

MY FRIEND, _____, AND HOW HE/SHE WAS AN UNCONDITIONALLY GREAT FRIEND TO ME:

_____
_____
_____
_____
_____
_____

RWE: "It is one of the blessings of old friends that you can afford to be stupid with them."

Aren't we lucky in that regard? We can act like complete idiots with our friends, and they will still love us. Think about how many times you went psycho crying to your friends about- let's face it… ridiculous stuff!! They did the same with us, and in the end, we all loved each other just the same. Why can't we be that forgiving with society? What might happen if we did forgive?

IF WE ALL FORGAVE SOCIETY FOR ITS STUPID BEHAVIORS, WHAT MIGHT HAPPEN TO THE WORLD?

_____
_____
_____
_____
_____
_____

HDT: "Friends…they cherish one another's hopes. They are kind to one another's dreams."

If you are a true friend, you will love and support your buddies and in all of their interests and passions. I have had three great friends since my childhood. Their names are Lisa, Amy, and Michelle. I have known Lisa since second grade, Amy since fourth grade, and Michelle since seventh. Now, I am 46 years old, which means that these friendships date back almost forty years! Do you know why this kinship is so sensationally strong? These girls have supported me and my pursuits since the day they met me. They are always encouraging me to take risks, chances, and to follow my pursuits with an unbridled passion! I love my girlfriends, and they love me back! I am blessed.

WHO ARE YOUR BEST BUDDIES, AND WHAT DO THEY DO TO SUPPORT YOU & YOUR DESIRES?

_____
_____
_____
_____
_____
_____

Carpe Diem (Seize the Day)

RWE: "Write it on your heart that every day is the best day in the year."

Live in the NOW. Celebrated speakers, philosophers, and thinkers have always known this. To live in the present moment is a gift. That is why it is called the "PRESENT." Screw the past, to hell with the future. You only have control of this day. What will you do with this moment? Write a book, as I am currently doing? Choose to exercise? Take a nap? It matters not what you do, as long as it feels right for you. Quit holding yourself hostage to the past (which, by the way, is gone). Cease fantasizing about the future. It's not here yet. Live for this current opportunity. Play some funky music. Dance. Come alive. How can you come alive right now? What will do it for you?

WAYS I CAN LIVE IN THIS MOMENT AND WHAT IT WILL DO FOR ME:

_____
_____
_____
_____
_____
_____

RWE: "With the past, I have nothing to do; nor with the future. I live NOW."

A lot of students gripe about their dysfunctional pasts. What they do not realize is that the more they drudge up the past, the more they hold themselves prisoners to it. Additionally, students fantasize so much about their lives coming around the corner, they forget to do the work in the present that will ensure a successful future. What principles/ideals do you want to live for today?

I WANT TO LIVE NOW FOR:

_____
_____
_____
_____

RWE: "This time, like all times, is a very good one, if we but know what to do with it."

Right now is a good time to do your best work, but most of us will not. We will get caught up in reminiscing about the past or dreaming of a brighter future. They key to success is to figure out what we can do with the time being, and really get something meaningful out of it. What should/could you be doing right now that would make you forget the past and ensure a successful future?

THINGS I SHOULD/COULD DO NOW TO HELP ENSURE SUCCESS IN THE FUTURE:

_____
_____
_____
_____
_____
_____

HDT: "Never look back unless you are planning to go that way."

Once again, the past is passed. You cannot go back and change or fix it. It is what it is. The real questions are, what did you learn from it, and how can you use that to solidify this moment? When you dwell too much on the earlier periods of your life, you expend too much time on something that will never be altered. If you do decide to go back in time, don't be surprised if you get stuck there like a person in quicksand. Slowly, but surely, you will sink deeper and deeper and become buried in the life you should be leaving behind.

WHAT PAST HURTS WILL YOU RELEASE TODAY? WHAT MIGHT THAT DO FOR YOUR WELL-BEING?

_____
_____
_____
_____
_____

Blaze Your Own Trail

RWE: Do not go where the path may lead, go instead where there is no path, and leave a trail."

Most people take the same path as everybody else, and forget to go their own way. Perhaps if they did elect to go in a different direction, they could change their miserable existences. At school each day, I see students wearing the same style clothes as everyone else, saying the same phrases they learned from their phones ("What are those!!!"), and behaving in a most similar and simplistic manner. It bothers me that they are afraid to come up with their own sense of style, their own creative catchphrases, and their own new ways of handling things. Perhaps if they did, they might feel a heck of a lot better than they currently do. Taking the same path down a common road will lead you to the masses. Are they happy? Think about it. Most people -especially teens- are depressed s.o.b.'s. Perhaps it is because they need to take a separate route. In what areas are you following the crowd, and how can you blaze a different trail?

WAYS I FOLLOW THE CROWD, AND HOW I CAN TAKE A DIFFERENT ROUTE:

_____
_____
_____
_____
_____
_____

HDT: "Live your beliefs and you can turn the world around."

Once again, follow your beliefs (as long as they are healthy), and you can make this world magical. Think about how many famous people followed their own original ideas, and they literally changed the world! These people moved mountains of injustice out of the way, invented technological advances beyond our comprehension, brought peace to war-torn nations, and not once did they stop and question their beliefs, because others did. They simply followed their ideas and hearts until they saw magnificent results. The rest, they say, is history." What are your beliefs, and how might they change the world?

MY AWESOME BELIEFS AND HOW THEY WILL CHANGE THIS PLANET:

_____
_____
_____
_____
_____
_____

Commitment

RWE: "Once you make a decision, the universe conspires to make it happen."

The "Other Side," no matter what you believe it to be, wants you to be successful. So you need to decide right now what you want to do with your life, and things will begin to unfold for you. A lot of my students think that they are victims of circumstance. They believe that life is happening to them- not for them. What they fail to recognize is that their lives are a reflection of what their decisions or indecisions have been. Life is not going to show up on your doorstep, and deliver you a roadmap to success. You have to get off your Apple Bottom jeans, and decide what it is you want, what it will take to get you there, and how you will feel when it comes. The Universe will come to your aid, but if, and only if, you make the commitment to do it. What do you want to decide to do right now?

I AM GOING TO COMMIT TO:

_____
_____
_____
_____

Dreams

HDT: "Dreams are the touchstones of one's character."

A touchstone is a judgment of something. In this case, your dreams indicate a lot to others about who you truly are. Think about people you know who have established no dreams for their future. What is your opinion or judgment of them? I would venture to guess that you don't hold them in high esteem. Are they interesting to you? Do you want to date or befriend them? Probably not. Now think of yourself. Do you have dreams? Have you named them? Out loud? On paper? Would people find you interesting if you had not established any fantasy goals for yourself? What dreams would you like to achieve today and in the future?

MY PRESENT AND FUTURE DREAMS:

___
___
___
___
___
___

HDT: "If one advances confidently in the direction of his dreams, and endeavors to live the life which he has imagined, he will meet with a success unexpected in common hours."

When you dream, you must do so with confidence and creativity. It will pay off. Do not dream by default. In other words, don't live on the hope that your fantasies will come to life. They simply won't. You have got to put a mega-strong belief in yourself in order to make the dreams become your reality. Your determination is key. You also need to be the absolute creator of these manifestations. Creatively visualize yourself going to that college. Immerse yourself in dorm life, the making of new friends, availability of money to pay for it, and the great grades and education you will receive from it. By constructing it in your mind, in your reality it will bind. (Hey, I am a poet, and I didn't know it!) The powers that be want to see that you are willing to see it as an actual part of your life, but it is up to you to do all of the pre-crafting. What do you want? How confident are you that it is already yours? How can you visualize it?

MY DREAMS, MY CONFIDENCE IN CREATING THEM, AND MY VISUALIZATION OF THEM:

___
___
___
___
___
___

Nature

RWE: "Nature always wears the colors of the spirit."

If you want to truly understand what is inside, look to nature. Nature has a lot of the answers, but many of us do not turn to her for guidance. Instead, we look to our technology or at others to help soothe our souls, but these do not help. That is because nature knows best. We need to give her a chance. She wants desperately to calm us and lift us, but we hear not her call. What metaphor (comparing 2 unlike things) can you come up with for nature?

NATURE IS A _____, BECAUSE:

_____
_____
_____
_____
_____
_____

RWE: "The sky is the daily bread of the eyes."

If you want nourishment for your soul, look again, to nature. There is so much beauty around you, but unless you stop to notice it, sadness will envelop you. When you get depressed, go for a walk. Look up at the sky, and try to find ways it links up with your inner being. This process alone should ease your worries a lot! Where, in nature, might you go to see the beauty of it? Remember what being in that spot did for you emotionally.

WHAT NATURAL SPOT BRINGS YOU PEACE? DESCRIBE IT IN GREAT DETAIL. WHAT DOES IT DO FOR YOU?

_____
_____
_____
_____
_____
_____

In my classroom, there are three squirrels who, every day, perch themselves upon the window sill- just waiting anxiously for a human snack (anything's got to be better than those stupid nuts). I cannot tell you how much joy these little buggers bring my students and me. We feed them Cheerios and fruit, and they absolutely love it. Sometimes, if the windows are open, they actually come inside, and sit in on a class. It is hilarious. We laugh, and take pictures of their beautiful fat selves (we aren't the only class who feeds them). The joy we get from their presence is undeniable. Animals are just a part of nature that we seriously need to stop and appreciate. It is though when they are around, all of our troubles melt away into a sea of sanity. Creatures bring a sense of clarity and calm that people cannot sometimes deliver. What animals do you love, and what do they do for your well-being?

ANIMALS I HAVE LOVED OR LOVE & WHAT THEY HAVE DONE TO ENHANCE MY BEING?

_____
_____
_____
_____
_____
_____

RWE: "The earth laughs in flowers.

Things get destroyed, deteriorate, die, but earth comes back with a sweet solution. She sprinkles the planet with an array of colors and petals to help lighten our loads of lament. Trees and flowers also offer us magnificent smells to inhale. What do you suppose is the value in such added colors and smells to our world? How might you use these gifts to grow emotionally?

THE BENEFIT OF PLANT LIFE or FLOWERS TO ME IS:

_____
_____
_____
_____
_____
_____

RWE: "Adopt the pace of Nature. Her secret is patience."

We can learn so much from Nature. She is one patient lady. She does not strain to grow her grass or trees. She simply allows the process to unfold. We spend so much of our time worrying about why things are not coming to us immediately. It could be love, opportunities, good grades, or happiness. If we were more patient, like Nature, we might not give up when life does not show up on our doorsteps so quickly. Chill out. Relax, and believe that it is yours, and it is on its way. It will come to you, as long as you exercise patience. About what are you most impatient, and how can you learn the art of waiting for it?

I HAVE A HARD TIME WAITING FOR_____, AND I CAN

LEARN TO WAIT FOR IT BY:

_____
_____
_____
_____
_____
_____

RWE: "If stars should appear but one night every thousand years, how man would marvel and stare."

We do not appreciate Nature the way we should. We take, for granted, Her marvels such as the moon and stars, but if we did not have frequent access to Her, we would appreciate these wonders much more. What are some aspects of Nature you appreciate and why? How can what we learn from Nature be applied to our own lives? What might happen if we did not take *anything* for granted? People? Places? Events?

WHAT I APPRECIATE IN NATURE & WHY?

_____
_____
_____
_____
_____
_____
_____

WHAT MIGHT HAPPEN IF WE DID NOT TAKE ANYTHING FOR GRANTED?

_____
_____
_____
_____
_____
_____
_____

RWE: "Nature hates calculators."

Nature does not wish to keep track of petty numbers. Nor should you.
As a society, we keep tabs on ridiculously minuscule details that have no bearing upon our happiness. For instance, we keep checklists of how many times people screw us over by their cheats, lies, betrayals, etc. Why do we wish to keep score? What is the point in all of the calculating? Why do we not just let it go? What does holding on to it do for us? What do you keep track of that is probably of no use to you?

I KEEP TRACK OF THESE STUPID THINGS:

_____
_____
_____
_____
_____
_____
_____

INSTEAD, I SHOULD BE KEEPING TRACK OF THESE IMPORTANT THINGS:

_____
_____
_____
_____
_____
_____
_____

HDT: Nature is full of genius, full of the divinity, so that not a snowflake escapes its fashioning hand."

Nature is one wicked smart lady. She designs things in her own perfect way. We have the same capabilities Nature possesses. Everything we touch has the potential to become gorgeous. We, like nature, have the gift of creating all sorts of fantastical things like snowflakes. Some of us dance, sing, play music, draw, speak, listen, exercise, cook, read, and write in the most unique ways. Like Nature, we have "fashioning hands." What are you good at, and how might you use your talents to design or do something dynamic?

MY TALENTS ARE:

_____
_____
_____
_____
_____
_____
_____,

AND THIS IS HOW I CAN USE THEM TO CREATE SOMETHING OF GREAT BEAUTY:

_____
_____
_____
_____
_____
_____
_____

Creativity

RWE: The creation of a thousand forests is in one acorn."

One nut (yes, YOU, ya crazy bastard!) has the potential to create something entirely vast. We are no different than acorns. As individuals, we are capable of doing so much. We doubt that our singular selves have the capacity to move mountains and save souls, but we are wrong in assuming this. If one acorn can do so much, why can't we?

THINGS LITTLE 'OL ME IS CAPABLE OF DOING:

_____
_____
_____
_____
_____
_____

HDT: "The world is but a canvas to our creativity."

This world was meant to paint, and you are its artist. When we look out at the planet, we see aspects of it we do not like or appreciate. We focus on the negative, nasty, non-nourishing parts. We need to understand that all it will take is for us to become creators of what we wish to see as an alternative. We can become agents of positivity, kindness, and love. We can do this by painting a different scene. This can be illustrated through our deeds, our words, and our perceptions. We can be designers of what we desire. How do you visualize the world to be? What colors and ideas about do you wish to paint?

I VISUALIZE THE WORLD TO BE A _____ PLACE. I WOULD

PAINT LOTS OF: _____

IN ORDER TO SEE THIS PLANET BECOME WHAT IT IS SUPPOSED TO BE.

IF I DID THIS, WE WOULD PROBABLY BEGIN TO NOTICE THAT

WAS POSSIBLE: _____

The Power of Self

RWE: Shallow men believe in luck. Strong men believe in cause and effect."

Don't rely on luck to get you where you need to go. You must initiate the change you wish to see in your life. I, like so many others, wished for a winning lottery ticket. Little did I know, I was holding one the entire time! It is I who is a winning ticket. I am worth millions. My ideas are worthwhile. It is I who needed to pursue these ideas. No luck was headed my way. I needed to create opportunity for ME! That is why I am writing this book. It WILL cause people to change, and whether or not money comes from it, I worry not. I rest peacefully in the knowledge that I will have given teens priceless tools and tips about enlightening themselves and their world. That, in itself is a most profitable earning! You, too, are in control of how much cause and effect you can create. What you do, or do NOT do, has a result. What kinds of results do you wish to see? Good or bad? The choice is yours. Choose wisely.

RESULTS I'D LIKE TO SEE FOR MYSELF:

_____
_____
_____
_____
_____
_____

The Help

RWE: "It is one of the beautiful compensations in this life that no one can sincerely try to help another without helping himself."

Your primary goal in this life should be to focus on developing YOU! You are the most important thing in your life, and without devotion to your own growth, you are of no use to others. Why not start a list right now of what you want to work on, and execute it? What do you ultimately want to give others? Are you giving it to yourself?

WHAT I WANT TO GIVE OTHERS:

_____
_____
_____
_____
_____
_____
_____

WHAT I GIVE MYSELF:

_____
_____
_____
_____
_____
_____
_____

Let's explore this quote once again:

RWE: "It is one of the beautiful compensations in this life that no one can sincerely try to help another without helping himself."

Easy to say, but not easy to do. We rely on others for our happiness, and yet we cannot. It does not work that way. One must devote his life entirely to the art of helping himself physically, spiritually, and emotionally, before he can even begin to think of assisting his outer circles of influence. Working on you is of the utmost importance. What can you do today to make changes in your life that will keep you happy and healthy?

CHANGES I CAN AND NEED TO MAKE:

_____
_____
_____
_____
_____
_____
_____

RWE: "Nothing is at least sacred but the integrity of your own mind."

Your mind is such a prize. Treat is as such. Keep your thoughts in a state of perpetual positive movement. Direct your ideas toward beauty, love, and individuality, and you cannot go wrong.

IN WHAT DIRECTION DO YOUR THOUGHTS TEND TO GO? HOW CAN YOU TRAIN YOUR IDEAS TO LEAD YOU DOWN A MORE POSITIVE PATH?

_____
_____
_____
_____

RWE: "What we seek we shall find; what we flee from flees from us."

Whatever you are looking for, you will find it. This is the absolute truth. If you look for trouble, you will find it. If you look for opportunity, you will discover it. Think about teachers you have had. Those who constantly look for what the students are doing wrong always find it! It is as though they thrive on locating negative behaviors! These people's classrooms are in a state of constant chaos. What they seek, they shall find. On the contrary, instructors who look for the best in kids, find IT! Avoid that which you do not wish to experience by not giving it thought or desire, and it will run from you. What do you seek? From where are you running?

I SEEK (GOOD OR BAD):

_____
_____
_____
_____
_____
_____
_____

AND IT APPEARS FOR ME.

I RUN FROM:

_____
_____
_____
_____
_____
_____
_____

AND IT FINDS ME.

FROM NOW ON, I AM GOING TO SEEK _____,

AND NEVER RUN FROM _____.

RWE: "We are wiser than we know."

This is simple. You are one smart cookie, and you do not give yourself credit for it! I have so many students in my classes who say and think they are not intelligent. That's Bolshevik, and I think they know it. It is merely a cop-out to not have to work hard. Ironically, though, they grow into adults who resent the successful people around them. All they had to do was believe in their intellects and talents, and they could have gone, far, but they chose to think they were stupid, and well, "Stupid is as stupid does." What do you tell yourself about your intellect?

I CONSTANTLY TELL MYSELF I AM:
_____

HOW IS THAT WORKING OUT FOR ME?
_____
_____
_____

I CAN CHANGE THIS BY TELLING MYSELF THAT I AM:
_____

ONCE I DO THIS, MY LIFE WILL GET:_____

HDT: "Do what you love. Know your own bone; gnaw at it, bury it, unearth it, and gnaw it still."

Yep. You know what you love to do (and I am not talking about sleeping or eating here). :) Name what you love to do, chew on it for a while, put it away for a few days, rediscover it, and chew on it some more. Share your gift with others. You can change people with your passions!
In my writing this book right now, I can see that it is a great passion of mine. I have always wanted to write a book which could change the world, and here I am doing it. I sometimes walk away from the computer, give myself time to think, revisit the manuscript, and then revert back to more idea-generating. Ultimately, this book will change the lives of others, but for now, it is my love bone that I will know, gnaw, bury, unearth, and gnaw at still. What is your bone?

MY BONE IS:
_____
_____
_____
_____
_____
_____

Beauty

RWE: "Love of beauty is taste. The creation of beauty is art."

So, if you worship other people or items, that is considered your "taste" in such things, but if you create your own beauty, which is considered "art." Why so many students feel the need to be copy-cats of one another is beyond my understanding. I suppose you can feel you have a certain taste for specific styles, but if a person truly wants to experience REAL beauty, then he/she must create that flair for him/herself.

WHAT BEAUTIFUL WORKS OF ART HAVE YOU CREATED?
_____
_____

_____
_____
_____
_____

RWE: "Though we travel the world over to find the beautiful, we must carry it with us or we find it not."

Beauty lies within you not outside of you. You can travel thousands of miles in search of gorgeousness, but you will not find it until you see it contained within you.

I FEEL _____ ABOUT MY INNER BEAUTY. THIS

BELIEF HAS GOTTEN ME_____.

WAYS I CAN MAINTAIN OR ELIMINATE THIS BELIEF ARE TO:

_____
_____
_____
_____
_____
_____
_____

RWE: "Never lose an opportunity to see anything beautiful, for beauty is in God's handwriting."

Look for beauty, and you shall find it. Whether you wish to see it or not-this world is a gorgeous place. Every day at work, I walk through the halls of my high school and try to perceive every person I encounter as a work of art. Sure, there are people who are annoying, mean, and sad, but I try to see them as gorgeous creatures of sad circumstance. They are suffering, or they wouldn't act in those manners, so I try to build them up, by smiling at them and offering them a glimmer of hope that happiness is indeed a possibility, but that it is for sure a choice! Usually, my students feel loved and appreciated by me, because I elect to see their merit. When they know my acknowledgement of their value is legit, they feel more inclined to share it with the rest of the world. It makes me feel good to help others see their true charm. It will make you feel good too. What do you see that is gorgeous in this world? How can our focusing on beauty help shape our perception the world?

I SEE BEAUTY IN:

_____
_____
_____
_____
_____
_____

IF I CONTINUE TO FOCUS ON THIS BEAUTY, MY PERCEPTION OF THE WORLD WILL:

_____
_____
_____
_____

HDT: "Heaven is under our feet as well as over our heads."

Everywhere you look, a heavenly beauty exists.
We need to stop looking at the world through such a dark lens, and begin to see a light of love that could illuminate the entire planet. The problem is, we are not looking in the right places for beauty to emerge. We look at ugly situations, the grotesque actions of others, and we see no eloquence. We need to seek life's treasures and place our attention upon principles such as truth, love, and compassion if we want to see the real glamour of humanity. How is Heaven under your feet and over your head?

HEAVEN IS UNDER MY FEET IN PLACES LIKE:

___

HEAVEN IS OVER MY HEAD IN PLACES LIKE:

___

Temptation

RWE: "We gain the strength of the temptation we resist."

Let's face it, we get stronger by resisting what is bad for us. I know sometimes I want to grab for that extra Dunkin' Doughnut, but I know that if I do, my butt will grow exponentially larger than it already is. When we resist the urge to take what we do not need, we grow! Think about all of the temptations in your life you could have resisted: bad people, bad circumstances, bad food, bad drugs/alcohol, poor choices. Now, imagine how empowered you would be if you had not given in to those temptations. How might your life be different? Do you like what you see? Good, then keep electing to resist those things you did in the past, and watch your life unfold in a direction far more positive than the life that came before it.

TEMPTATIONS I GAVE IN TO:

_____
_____
_____

RESULTS OF MY CHOICES:
_____
_____
_____
_____
_____
_____

WHAT MIGHT HAVE HAPPENED IF I DIDN'T CAVE IN TO THE TEMPTATIONS:
_____
_____
_____
_____
_____

Mind Your Own Business

RWE: "Little minds have little worries. Big minds have not time for worries."

Some people choose to worry about stupid crap, and better minds do not take the time to even think about minor details. Of which mind are you? Little or Big? How is that working out for you? Do you want to spend the rest of your days sweating out the small stuff, or do you want to be truly free by only concentrating on issues that are of the utmost importance such as health, happiness, family, education, and fun? Do you want to petty yourself with other people's details and problems, or do you want to focus on the main purpose for your being here: YOU- the development of YOU! We spend so much of our time worrying about all of the rest of the world and its silly dramas. Hell, we Tweet about it, Facebook about it, Snapchat about it, and for what? Where is the value? We need to abandon society's ridiculous ills, and begin to create a life of love for ourselves. Can you do it? Can you mind your own business literally and figuratively? I hope so. You'll be glad you did!

I HAVE A MIND FOR:
_____
_____
_____
_____
_____

Get 'Er Done

RWE: "The reward of a thing well done is having done it."

"Just Do It." That is Nike's advice. Now when are you going to listen to it? We need to jump into life's game, and play it. Problem is, we don't. We sit around our houses, watching television, playing video games, viewing posts made by others, and we neglect to play our own game. It's called LIFE. We really need to become participants. We need to "Get 'Er Done." Every June and July, I teach summer school. Each year, it is the same situation; kids are here who decided **_not_** to "Get 'Er Done." It saddens me to know that all they had to do was work in their classes from September until June, and then they would be out speeding around on bodacious boats, or soaking up the sensational sun rays, but no, they are here with me in school- trying to make up credits they lost for not following that golden rule: You guessed it; Gettin' 'Er Done!." What a pity it is. Just think the regrets they have. If they would have just stayed focused for nine months, they would not be in this situation. It truly saddens me. We all put off things we do not like or want to do, but in the end, it catches up with us, and ultimately damages our lives in ways we mostly regret. What do you need to get done? What might happen if you do it now? What might happen if you don't?

I NEED TO GET THE FOLLOWING DONE:

_____
_____
_____
_____
_____
_____
_____

IF I "GET 'ER DONE" NOW, THE FOLLOWING MIGHT HAPPEN:

_____
_____
_____
_____
_____
_____
_____

IF I DON'T "GET 'ER DONE" NOW, THE FOLLOWING MIGHT HAPPEN:

_____
_____
_____
_____
_____
_____

THEREFORE, GETTING THE CRAP DONE I LISTED ABOVE IS A DAMN GOOD IDEA.

Fight the Good Fight

RWE: "When we quarrel, how we wish we'd been blameless."

Every fight you have with others is a result of both parties' engagement. If you are arguing with someone else, do you understand that you can simply walk away or disengage? Most times, we do not think this is an option. We simply feel we are in a hostage crisis, and these people are not going to let go of their chokehold on us, because it is pleasurable for them to see us have to defend our points. Guess what, People? You do not have to defend yourself to or for anyone (unless you are in a court of law)! You can exercise the right to remove yourself from the situation, and trust me, you will be glad you did. You know why? Because now you cannot be blamed! Don't get me wrong, some things are worth fighting for. The question is- what? What fights do you wish you would have abandoned? What is/was worth fighting for?

I WISH I WOULD HAVE LEFT THE FIGHT WITH _____, BECAUSE:
_____

A FIGHT WORTH MY STAYING INVOLVED IN WOULD HAVE BEEN WITH:
_____

BECAUSE:_____

Aim High

RWE: Hitch your wagon to a star."

Set your goals super high. Sounds easy enough, doesn't it? Sadly, most of us believe our pursuits are out of reach. Because of this negative mindset, we ask the bare minimum of ourselves, and guess what we get? Bare minimal results! We need to push for passionate possibilities! We must come to realize that the larger aspirations we set for ourselves will be equal to the amount of success we will have in the future. If we set our expectations low, we will achieve little to nothing. When have you set your intentions up for failure? How did you like the results? What lofty ambitions can you set for yourself today?

WHEN I HAVE SET MY GOALS SHALLOWLY, THE FOLLOWING HAS HAPPENED:
_____

MY SUPERB AMBITIONS ARE TO:
_____

_____

WHEN I ACHIEVE THESE, I WILL LEARN:

_____
_____
_____
_____
_____

RWE: Unless you try to do something beyond what you already have mastered, you will never grow."

We all know what we are good at. The question is, "Are you willing to learn something new? "If you aren't, you probably will never grow. We are all creatures of absolute habit. We think we need to keep playing the same games, dating the same types of people, expecting the same of ourselves each day, but this is not contributing to our enlightenment. We are in a constant state of complacency. It is not healthy. We need to branch out and learn more in all areas of our lives- especially physically, spiritually, intellectually, and emotionally. We need to read new books, explore different places, study other religions, ride different bikes, and date different types of people. It will truly help us grow. Isn't that the point to our being here- to evolve? Yes, it is! What have you not tried yet that you would like to? How might that help you to grow?

I WOULD LIKE TO TRY:

_____
_____
_____
_____
_____
_____

IF I TRIED THESE THINGS, THIS MIGHT HAPPEN:

_____
_____
_____
_____
_____
_____

HDT: "Live the life you've dreamed."

You are the creator of YOUR life. Every day that you wake up, you have a new chance to design your life the way you want it to be. How do you want it to go? I am hoping you selected the adverb, "MAGNIFICENTLY!" If so, then you are on your way to building a bigger and better dream for your existence. If you can dream it; you can make it become a reality. A lot of people will say that is a receptacle of rubbish, but I am here to tell you it is no myth. The world's wisest have always known this. As much as we want to deny ourselves the passionate possibilities, they are ours for the taking! When will you carpe diem (seize the day), and understand the power that exists within you can design the life you have dreamed of for years? How about NOW?

MY DREAM LIFE WOULD BE:

_____
_____
_____
_____
_____

I CAN BEGIN TO BRING THIS LIFE "TO LIFE" BY:

_____
_____
_____
_____
_____
_____

Community

RWE: Our best thoughts come from others."

We learn a lot of valuable ideas from everybody. Therefore, we should take note, and implement them. I feel that the best type of learning takes place in groups, where people are working as collaborators on tasks. Most schools force kids to work in isolation, and this is not healthy or productive. We need to take the time to share our thoughts and ideas on topics which warrant our attention, and one way to do that is to work in teams. Working with others gives one a sense of unity and responsibility. It can be a great way to grow as a thinker, learner, and speaker. Think of a time in your life, when you worked on a project with others that went really well. What factors went into the success of that cooperative effort?

TIMES I WORKED WITH OTHERS, AND IT WENT REALLY WELL:

_____
_____
_____
_____
_____
_____

RWE: "Make yourself necessary to somebody."

In order to feel valued, we need to help people. A lot of times, we are so driven to take care of ourselves, and we do so really well, but we still feel empty inside. This is because it is not always about us. We are all connected- spiritually, emotionally, physically, and intellectually, and when there is a break in that connectedness, we feel lost. Well guess what? We **should** feel lost. We aren't in this game alone- we are in it together! Go ahead, and make yourself necessary to another. Hell, make yourself necessary to a lot of people! It is a game-changer both for you and society. To whom are you currently necessary? How has your presence in their life been beneficial?

I AM NECESSARY TO_____, BECAUSE I HELP

HIM/HER/THEM:
_____
_____
_____
_____
_____
_____

RWE: "The reason why the world lacks unity and lies broken and in heaps, is because man is disunited with himself."

If you don't like you, you are screwing this world out of absolute goodness! I have witnessed a lot of dysfunctional people in my life, and do you know what they all have in common? They hate themselves. These are your jealous, sad, angry people. They wake up every day with a giant chip of self-disdain on their shoulders, but instead of getting off their angry butts and changing the direction of their lives, they simply find ways to create misery in other people's experiences. This, my friends, is disuniting our world. It is why we have wars, divorces, playground fights, rapes, murders, robberies, etc. People are not willing to unite their outer and inner cores of being, so they live in a state of perpetual misery- which they cannot stand to be in alone, so they rope the rest of us in by being critical jerks and bullies, in order to make themselves feel less alone. When someone once said, "Misery loves company," I assure you they were right. Misery is a dastardly diva of destruction. She will not rest until she has an astronomically large audience and following. We must not succumb to her whims. What might happen if each person were able to abandon his self-loathing? What might happen to humanity?

IF PEOPLE LOVED THEMSELVES MORE, OUR COMMUNITIES WOULD CHANGE BY:
_____
_____
_____
_____
_____
_____

RWE: "Our chief want is someone who will inspire us to be what we know we could be."

When I was in 7th grade, I was going through a lot of tough times. I was acting up a lot at home and failing most of my classes. My mom sent me to various psychologists and psychiatrists to try to "fix me." It did not work. Then, my friend, Lisa M. asked me if I want to go see a motivational speaker with her mom and her. Reluctantly, I went, and surprisingly, it changed my life. The man's name was Michael Wickett, and when he spoke, something inside me changed. I had never had anyone tell me that the design of my life was entirely up to me. This concept seemed so foreign. After all, I thought life was this nightmare orchestrated by some higher power- hell-bent on destroying me. Little did I know, before listening to Mr. Wickett, that it was I who held all of the power. After his presentation, I made a concerted effort to change my reality. It worked! My life slowly started to turn around, once I realized I held the keys to unlocking my own success, but you see, I needed Michael Wickett to inspire me. Who has inspired you? In what ways?

_____ (INSERT COOL PERSON HERE)

HAS INSPIRED ME IN THE FOLLOWING WAYS:

_____
_____
_____
_____
_____
_____
_____

Meditation

RWE: "Let us be silent, that we may hear the whispers of the gods."

If we want peace, we need to be silent. In a crazy, super-charged world filled with technology, people, and numerous responsibilities, it is nearly impossible to get an ounce of serenity in our lives. We, however, have got to find a way. It is an ultimate source of tranquility that will lead us to a promise of a better today and tomorrow. We should take time to build silence into our daily routines. There should be a designated ½ hour of stillness each day which enables our bodies, minds, and souls to recharge. Without it, we are cheating ourselves from hearing, as Ralph Waldo Emerson puts it, "the whispers of the gods." What time of the day do you have free? Where would/could you go to meditate? What might this quiet time do to change your inner being?

I COULD SET UP A TIME TO MEDITATE FROM_____ TO _____

I WOULD GO TO _____ TO MEDITATE.

DOING THIS WOULD PROBABLY: _____ ME.

Health

RWE: "The first wealth is health."

Health is a hot commodity. Let's face this fact; if you don't have health, you have nothing. It is a gift you give yourself to eat healthy, sleep well, and exercise much. Most teens are not taking care of themselves, and it is affecting many areas of their lives- especially their school lives. As a teacher, I see it every day- kids super exhausted, sleeping in class, and looking like garbage. It is definitely from a lack of sleep. When I inquire about it, they simply say they stayed up too late playing video games, watching television, or playing on their phones. They cannot see a correlation between their poor sleep patterns and their hideous performance and appearance at school. People, YOU NEED TO SLEEP! What part of that do you not understand??? Additionally, kids come to school hungry each morning, and this makes them grumpy. They do not have any energy in their bodies, so this, too, leads to much exhaustion and apathy. As mentioned above, kids are not exercising as much either, and this leads to a sabotaging sluggishness which changes the learning dynamic as well. You have got to regain your health, if you want to feel the wealth. When would NOW be a good time to reassess your health habits?

MY SLEEPING HABITS _____,
BECAUSE_____.

MY EATING HABITS_____,
BECAUSE_____.

MY EXERCISE HABITS_____.
BECAUSE_____.

MY GOALS REGARDING:

SLEEPING: _____

EATING: _____

EXERCISE: _____

Opportunity Knocks

RWE: "Every wall is a door."

Quit looking at obstacles as barriers. They are gateways. I am 46 years old, and when I look back on all of the years that I graduated with the most growth, it was when things really sucked. At the time, I resented the crap out of those moments of misery, but I learned that in those times of turmoil, the universe had set me up to experience what would become my most meaningful opportunities for advancement. As a little kid and teen, I had a hard life. Basically, I grew up hating most of the world and everything in it. Little did I know that out of my greatest doom would come my greatest lessons- lessons I would take into my career as a mom, teacher, motivational speaker, actress, and writer. People, without these unsavory times, I would not have grown into the wonderful human that I am today. These negative moments have taught me to experience and create continuous compassion, unconditional love, fantastic fun, and unlimited potential. What obstacles have you faced that were probably just disguised as opportunities?

I CAN NOW SEE THAT WHEN I WENT THROUGH THE FOLLOWING EXPERIENCES:

_____

_____

_____

THEY WERE JUST GATEWAYS TO MY LEARNING ABOUT:

_____

RWE: "No great man ever complains of want of opportunity."

Successful people see opportunity everywhere. If we could all just understand that magical moments are at our disposal constantly, there would simply be no limit to what resources we could tap. You have got to wake up, and see how incredibly abundant opportunities are there for the taking. We can be whomever it is we desire. We can get whatever it is we desire. We can pursue whomever it is we desire. We can accomplish whatever it is we desire. If it is to be, it is up to YOU. I have been believing this for about the past ten years. I wanted to be a motivational speaker, so I found a way. I wanted to be an actress, so I found a way. I wanted to write this book, so I found a way. I wanted to make more money, so I found a way. I wanted to meet a great guy, so I found a way. Notice all of the "I's" listed. Nobody "wanted" for me. I created a desire, sought it intently, and BAM, it manifested! Opportunities are there for the taking, but you need to name what you want, hotly pursue it, and never give up until it is yours. The possibilities are endless.

THE OPPORTUNITIES I WOULD LIKE TO SEE KNOCKING AT MY DOOR ARE:

_____

THESE OPPORTUNITIES WILL MOST LIKELY COME IF I:

_____

Love

RWE: "All mankind love a lover."

We should love loving people. If we are an evolved group of beings, then we will most likely embrace those who love. If most of your life is spent in absolute awe and respect for humanity, then you are doing something right, and it will love you back. It is the people who despise humanity who live such a miserable experience. They cannot see the glory of love and all of its healing qualities. Love, if you have ever felt it, is a magnificent source of harmony and tranquility that is insurmountable by any other concept. When it enters you, there is no way it can destroy. It has a magnificent magnetism, which, when used to help oneself and others, has the potential to heal entire entities. Did you ever wonder why it is so hard to hate a loving person? That is because the strength of love far outweighs anything that tries to slay it. With this knowledge, why would you not want an unlimited supply of love to fill your every fiber? Don't you want that kind of positive control? In what ways do you show your love to others? How has that helped them? How has that helped you?

I SHOW MY LOVE BY:

_____
_____
_____
_____
_____
_____
_____

THIS HAS HELPED OTHERS BY:

_____
_____
_____
_____
_____
_____
_____

MY SHOWING LOVE HAS HELPED ME BY:

_____
_____
_____
_____
_____
_____
_____

Judgment

HDT: "It is never too late to give up our prejudices."

We can stop judging today. Up until now, we have held beliefs about specific groups. Chances are, those beliefs were taught to you by another. That is what makes them wrong. You need to abandon everything prejudice you have heard, seen, or been taught, and start anew. Let go of the debilitating belief that your ideas or ways of doing things are superior to another's. This is just unhealthy. It is never too late to open up your heart and embrace humankind for what it is- an absolute beauty. We are inclined to judge, because it makes us feel a false sense of power over others, but indeed it is a FALSE sense. It is so wrong to want to isolate others from our realm of influence. Remember, we are a team here. As a species, we work better together-not separate. Once we begin to realize and capitalize on this idea, we can truly evolve as beings. Whom do you judge? Why is that not fair? From where did you learn to judge others? How might NOT judging others change your experience?

I MOSTLY JUDGE:

_____
_____
_____
_____
_____
_____
_____

THIS IS NOT FAIR, BECAUSE:

_____
_____
_____
_____
_____
_____
_____

I LEARNED TO JUDGE OTHERS FROM:

_____
_____
_____
_____
_____
_____
_____

IF I STOPPED JUDGING, MY EXPERIENCE WOULD CHANGE BY:

_____
_____
_____
_____
_____
_____
_____

RWE: "There are other measures of self-respect for a man than the number of clean shirts he puts on every day."

Our clothes do not define us. Why do we place so much value on the way people dress and look? When we die, are we going to be able to take those designer labels to the grave with us? I think not. We will be remembered for our contributions to this game of life. We will be remembered for how we treated people and by what we taught them. The expensive winter coat we sport or the athletic shoes we step into each day do not define us. Our actions do. We are members of a society who likes to judge people on what they do and do not have. It is not healthy for us to do so, for it is what separates us from one another in ways that are not conducive to peace and understanding. I know many people who do not dress well who are magnificent people. On the contrary, I know people who dress really well who are rude, angry, and judgmental. Does how a person dresses change your opinion about them? Why?

EXPLAIN WHETHER OR NOT YOU GIVE PEOPLE MORE RESPECT WHO DRESS WELL:
_____
_____
_____
_____
_____
_____
_____

WHY DO YOU DO THIS?
_____
_____
_____
_____
_____
_____
_____

RWE: "There is an optical illusion about every person we meet."

What you see in others is not necessarily real. When you see or meet people, you automatically assume that they are what the eyes perceive. This, of course, is not the case. There is so much depth to humanity that cannot always been seen, heard, or even felt. We have to dig deeper. How many times have you seen a girl dressed in skimpy shorts and made an assumption that she was easy? How many times have you seen a person with crooked teeth and assumed they were poor or dirty? Every day, in a myriad of ways, we judge people for the optical illusion we see. This is not who these people are. This is just your judgmental mind wanting to ascribe meaning to what you think to be the truth, when indeed, it is not. Whom have you mislabeled in the past? Who were they really, and how did you uncover the truth?

I ONCE MIS-JUDGED A PERSON NAMED_____. I FOUND OUT:
_____
_____
_____
_____
_____
_____

Interpretation

HDT: It's not what you look at that matters, it's what you see."

We do not always see the truth of what is going on, but oftentimes, that is our choice.

You see, we choose to see things as we wish to view them. We can look at a person or a situation, and come to an immediate conclusion about it- that may or may not necessarily be right. What we need to do is to take the time to ask ourselves what we are looking for. For instance, in my years as a teacher, I have noticed that a lot of other teachers go out of their way to look for kids causing trouble, and guess what? They always find it. I, however, look for what kids are doing right in my classroom, and guess what else? I always find *it*!

What do you choose to see? What does that say about you?

I CHOOSE TO SEE:

_____
_____
_____
_____
_____
_____
_____

WHAT DOES THAT SAY ABOUT YOU?

_____
_____
_____
_____
_____
_____
_____
_____

RWE: 'Nature and books belong to the eyes that see them."

In nature, I might notice a tree's withering brown leaves, while you might observe its strongly rooted trunk. I might pay attention to impending rain, while you might note the light through the clouds. When we read, I might notice a character as being amazingly heroic, while you might identify her as villainous. I might notice the action of the plot, while you might notice the psychological motives of the characters. Like nature and books, our interpretation of life's offerings is subjective, and it should be. No two people's perspectives can be entirely identical, and that is why it is so important that you let go of this egoic belief that your version is the "only" way to see. All of us have the right to view situations from our own unique perspective. It is healthy for humanity to allow us to do so.

WHEN YOU LOOK OUT IN NATURE, WHAT DO YOU SEE?

_____
_____
_____
_____
_____

WHAT MIGHT THIS MEAN?

_____
_____
_____
_____

WHEN YOU READ A BOOK, WHAT DO YOU NOTICE FIRST?

WHAT MIGHT THIS MEAN?

WHEN YOU LOOK OUT AT LIFE, WHAT DO YOU SEE?

WHAT MIGHT THIS MEAN?

Talking Smack

RWE: "Use what language you will. You can never say anything but what you are."

You are what you speak. Do not ever underestimate the power of your talk. Whatever is constantly coming out of your mouth will become your reality. For example, if you are repeatedly complaining about how rotten life is, your life will become more rotten. This is because energy goes where attention flows. If you are always talking about other people, be sure to check yourself, and try to figure out if what you are calling them is actually what you are. This is called "projection." This is where a person actually "projects" his or her own inadequacies onto someone else. It is a really bad habit for a person to get into, because it is counterproductive. It alienates you from the subject of your judgment, and it does not build what

I like to call a relationship bridge. Your goal should not be to talk smack, but it should be to love back.

ABOUT WHOM HAVE YOU SPOKEN SMACK, AND HOW HAS THAT BEEN BENEFICIAL? TO THEM? TO YOU?

_____
_____
_____
_____
_____
_____

This next one is very similar, but says so even better:

RWE: "People do not seem to realize that their opinion of the world is also a confession of their character."

YOU are THAT which you love or hate.

How's that for a nice companion piece? Speaking of Peace...

Peace

RWE: "The real and lasting victories are those of peace, and not of war."

We are not victorious when we "win a war." We are victors when we achieve peace.
I see kids at my school fight sometimes, and they think it is really cool. Sometimes, they have even videotaped it with their phones, and have proceeded to show multitudes of people how they "beat the crap outta someone." They do not realize that this does not make them winners. It makes them losers. Any time you are seeking out ways to harm humanity, you are not a winner. You are a loser. You are simply contributing to the breakdown of society. Your main aim in life should be to create tranquility. It is why we are here. Harmony is the answer. What was the question?

IN WHAT WAYS CAN/DO YOU PROMOTE PEACE?

_____
_____
_____
_____
_____
_____

RWE: "Nobody can bring you peace but yourself."

We always think, "Well, if I had this person, or this job, or this amount of money in the bank," it could generate a sense of calm, but nothing outside of yourself has that grand potential. My friends, it is YOU who holds the keys to inner calm. Nothing outside of your inner being can deliver the serenity you deserve. It is ONLY you who can relieve the stressors. How can you locate the peace?

I CAN FIND PEACE WITHIN MYSELF BY:
_____
_____
_____
_____
_____

Attempting New Tasks

RWE: "All life is an experiment. The more experiments you make the better."

The more we try, the less we die. We have to get off our couches, off our phones, and out of our beds, and really try new adventures. This could mean our trying out new foods, clothing styles, cityscapes, friendships, attitudes. It matters not what we are doing, as long as we are not doing the same routine every day. We are not wired that way. We were born for adventure, and we need to embrace every opportunity to explore. What experiments await you? How might these endeavors enhance your life?

I REALLY NEED TO EXPERIMENT WITH (keep it clean):
_____
_____
_____
_____
_____
_____

IF I EXPLORED MORE AVENUES, MY LIFE WOULD SURELY:
_____
_____
_____
_____
_____

Be Nice

RWE: "You cannot do a kindness too soon, for you never know how soon it will be too late."

Don't put off doing something sweet for someone. Do it NOW! We were born to be nice. Do you know how I know that? Every time I am kind to someone, it makes me feel really fantastic. Every time I am mean to someone, it feels bad. So the question I must ask myself is, "Do I want to feel like garbage, or do I want to feel awesome?" Of course, I want to feel awesome, so I choose being loving. It works every time. This must be why I am always in a great mood. I do not want to hurt anyone, and you know what? Most people do not want to hurt me as a result of it. Hurt people hurt people. I am not hurt, so I do not hurt.

TO WHOM HAVE YOU SHOWN KINDNESS LATELY?
_____
_____
_____

HOW DID THAT MAKE YOU FEEL?
_____
_____
_____

WHEN HAVE YOU ELECTED TO BE MEAN?
_____
_____
_____

HOW DID *THAT* MAKE YOU FEEL?
_____
_____
_____

Embrace & Give of Yourself

RWE: "Make the most of yourself, for that is all there is of you."

You have got to start seeing yourself as having boundless potential for absolute greatness. You are the gift you give yourself. Now go ahead, unwrap you, and see the magnificent present you are to YOU. What attributes do you possess that could transform this world into a better place? How might you heal others with your gifts of strength? You are all you've got, so start digging yourself. Have you noticed how cool you are lately? Do you even have a gosh darn clue what a masterpiece your mind, body and soul are? Hello!!! I am not joking! Dude, once you realize the beauty of you, you can be or do anything you please! When would today be a good day to start embracing yourself?

IF I WERE TO MAKE THE MOST OF MYSELF, I WOULD REALIZE THAT I AM:
_____
_____
_____
_____

IF MOST PEOPLE WITNESSED THE ME THAT IS ME, I COULD SHAPE THIS WORLD BY:
_____
_____

_____
_____
_____

RWE: "The greatest gift is a portion of yourself."

Let's face it, we all have talents. Isn't it time you share yours with the rest of the planet? Come on, we are waiting. Where are those abilities hiding, and when are you going to let us be influenced by them? I have students who are phenomenal artists, speakers, writers, thinkers, and listeners. All of their aptitudes combine to contribute a dynamism to my class that is unsurpassed. Each student's contribution is necessary to sustain a higher level of learning. We all work together, with our presents, to create presence.

WHAT GIFTS DO YOU POSSESS?

_____
_____
_____
_____
_____
_____

HOW DO YOUR GIFTS BRING ADDED VALUE TO YOURSELF AND THE LIVES OF OTHERS?

_____
_____
_____
_____
_____
_____

Do Your Best

"A man is relieved and gay when he has put his heart into his work and done his best; but what he has said or done otherwise shall give him no peace."

Hey, you can say what you did was great, or even pretend that it was, but in the end, when you do **_not_** do your best, you know it, and it will not deliver you any solace. You should always be aiming to do your best- whatever the endeavor. When I was your age, I waited tables at two different restaurants. I wanted to be the greatest waitress the two establishments had ever hired. I always showed up for work early, never asked to depart early, and slopped food down on people's tables faster than any of the other servers. I simply wanted to be the best, and it literally paid off. Oftentimes, I would make much more money than the other workers. You see, I learned at a very young age, that when you work harder than you thought you were capable of working, you can literally astonish yourself and everyone else. It pays to do your best. People will take notice, and reward you for it. Best of all, the reward you give yourself for having done such a phenomenal job with be plenty enough to keep you going for years to come.

CITE A TIME IN YOUR LIFE WHEN YOU DID YOUR ABSOLUTE BEST:

WHAT DID THAT DO FOR YOU EMOTIONALLY?

WHAT MIGHT HAPPEN TO THE WORLD IF WE ALL DECIDED TO DO OUR BEST?

Learning

RWE: "We are by nature observers, and thereby learners. That is our permanent state."

We are (and should always be) in a constant state of learning. We need to act as sponges-soaking up whatever information is what's best for the evolution of our souls. Let us continue to grasp this concept until the end of time. Earlier in this book, I told you that life was like a school, and that we needed to constantly learn as many lessons we could in order to accomplish our missions for being here.

SO FAR, WHAT ARE THE GREATEST LIFE LESSONS YOU HAVE LEARNED AND FROM WHOM OR WHERE DID YOU LEARN THEM?

WHY ARE THESE LESSONS IMPORTANT FOR YOU TO HAVE GRASPED, AND WITH WHOM SHALL **YOU** SOMEDAY SHARE THEM?

HDT: "I put a piece of paper under my pillow, and when I could not sleep, I wrote in the dark."

Your mind is constantly craving the experience of learning. Even when you try to go to sleep, your brain is working tirelessly to get you to create and remember more. When your head does this, by all means, record it! Don't let your ideas pass you by. Inspiration came to you for a reason, now chronicle it! Learning does not cease once you step out of your school building. It is happening everywhere- in home, outside in nature, at sporting events, at concerts, online, on your phone. Life is trying to deliver you lessons with every breath you take. Please be cognizant of that absolute fact, and ingest as much knowledge as you possibly can! You will not regret it!

IN WHAT WAYS CAN YOU CHRONICLE WHAT YOU HAVE LEARNED?

HOW MIGHT REMEMBERING IMPORTANT LEARNINGS ENHANCE YOUR LIFE?

Less is More

HDT: "Our life is frittered away with detail...simplify, simplify, simplify.

We have too much crap- too many clothes, too many gadgets, too many obligations. All this creates is *too* many problems! We need to lessen the load by ridding ourselves of all of the excess in our lives! If we would remove this unnecessary trash in our lives, we could truly be free. This goes for our lockers, our bedrooms, our cars, our computers, and even the toxic people- all of them- filled with needless junk.

WHAT EXCESS ITEMS COULD YOU RID YOURSELF OF TODAY?

WHAT MIGHT YOUR LIFE BE LIKE IF YOU WERE TO ABANDON THESE ITEMS OF CLUTTER? HOW WOULD YOU FEEL? (DO NOT ANSWER THIS IF YOU ARE A HOARDER!) LOL!

___

Technology's Perils

HDT: "Men have become tools of their tools."

Boy, did Henry David Thoreau "have it going on" when he said this! And to think, this was stated more than 200 years ago- way before most technological inventions were even conceived! Let's get real with ourselves; we are slaves to our technology. With our tools, we have become tools, and we are the technology's tools. They control and manipulate us. Why do we give technology such power over our lives? It is time to reclaim ourselves. We must not allow our lives to be ruled by robots! We are members of the human race, and we need to re-acclimate ourselves back into society. We spend inordinate amounts of time buried in our phones, our televisions, and online. In case you didn't notice yet, these acts of "tooling" are killing us as a society. We do not even have legitimate conversations with one another anymore. We are drifters- pulling away from what needs us most- ourselves and others. We must get out and see the world for all of its beauty. We must create the beauty, if it is no longer observable! We CANNOT be tools of our tools!

HOW MUCH TIME DO YOU SPEND WITH YOUR "TOOLS?"

___

HOW HAVE YOUR TOOLS DESTROYED YOUR RELATIONSHIPS?

___

WHAT NEW TOOLS COULD YOU REPLACE THE OLD ONES WITH?

___

Keep an Open Mind

"HDT: "Nay, be a Columbus to whole continents and worlds within you, opening new channels not of trade but of thought."

This is a fantastic metaphor for how to be an explorer of ideas- not just of places. We are sometimes a tad too set in our ways, and we need to open up to new people and ways of living and thinking, if we truly wish to evolve. Every being, as I have told you, has a gift. Why would you **not** want to meet as many cool people as you possibly could? You can learn so much from the others- how to do things, how to think about things, how to create things, and yet some of us choose to live lives of absolute isolation. How will we ever advance if we do not open our minds like parachutes, which, by the way, also only function when open. This world is a playground of opportunity. When will you begin to let the opportunities abound?

I CAN OPEN MY MIND UP IN THE FOLLOWING WAYS:

_____
_____
_____
_____
_____
_____

HDT: "The Universe is wider than our views of it."

We have very limited sight of who and what this Universe represents. We need to expand our thinking about it, and alter our perceptions to envelop a more positive expectation. We look to the world to constantly disappoint us, and that is what we are always going to find. Let us adopt an expectation of love and compassion, and perhaps that is what we experience more. We are victims of our perception, but we could be victors of our reception. The choice is yours. Which way will you go?

IF I CHOOSE TO SEE THE WORLD IN A NEGATIVE LIGHT, MY WORLD WILL:

_____
_____
_____
_____
_____

IF I CHOOSE TO SEE THE WORLD IN A POSITIVE LIGHT, MY WORLD WILL:

_____
_____

Speaking of Negative and Positive…
Negativity vs. Positivity

HDT: "There are a thousand hacking at the branches of evil to one who is striking at the root."

So many people are looking to hate on the haters and the hate, while others simply cut the two off at the roots, so that they never have the chance to grow in the first place. We need to address what starts the evil in the first place. This is the proactive thing to do. We will never change the world's disappointing ways with angry responses. We can only change them with love and kindness.

WHAT BRANCHES OF EVIL HAVE YOU BEEN HACKING AT LATELY?

_____
_____
_____
_____
_____
_____

WHAT ROOTS SHOULD YOU BE TRYING TO STRIKE AT INSTEAD?

_____
_____
_____
_____
_____
_____

RWE: "For every minute you remain angry, you give up 60 seconds of peace of mind."

We spend so much time pissed off at the world, we lose a lot of time that we could be sitting in a state of absolute bliss. Being enraged IS A CHOICE, People! You CAN choose otherwise. Why wouldn't you?

WHAT ARE YOU ANGRY ABOUT?

_____
_____
_____
_____
_____

WHAT MIGHT HAPPEN IF YOU CHOSE TO LET IT GO?

Expectations

HDT: "Men are born to succeed- not fail."

We are here to be achievers not flops, and yet so many people are not succeeding. Why? People are not afraid of failure; they are afraid of success. Hey, being successful takes a lot of hard work- hard work that most people are not willing to invest the time in contributing. A couple nights a week, I wait tables at a restaurant. I make pretty good money, while others do not. Ironically, I am 46, and most of the people I work with are in their early 20's. Their problem is they do not want to work hard. They always ask for their shifts to be cut early, they often call in sick, and they do not take the task-at-hand (serving others) very seriously. I, however, do. I show up for work early every day, stay focused on the customer at all times, and always volunteer to stay late and close the restaurant. Is it any wonder, then, why I make more money than everyone else? No. It is because I am willing to invest time and energy into being successful. You see, I know the secret; men are born to succeed- not fail." I do what I was born to do. Do you?

WHAT CAN YOU DO TODAY TO ENSURE YOUR OWN SUCCESS?

Rage Against the Machine

HDT: "Disobedience is the true foundation of liberty. The obedient must be slaves."

If we want to be free, we need not always obey. It does not always help in the development of our souls. Unfortunately, we have been taught to follow the commands. Obey the rules, obey your elders, obey authority. I suppose these are fine for managing people who need managing, but not always are rules, elders, or authority figures right. In fact, sometimes these people are just plain jerks. I am not going to tell you to entirely rage against the machine, but I am going to tell you that if something an adult asks you to do completely goes against your convictions, then by all means- do NOT do it! These people and their rules do not always have your best interest at heart. I am not instructing you to tell them to go "f" off. You can simply, and gently state, "I am not comfortable with what you are asking me to do, and I would like you to explain to me why this is considered necessary at this point in time." Don't be surprised if this pushes these "authority masters" over the veritable edge, but as long as you maintain your cool, things might turn out the way you like. You might help these authority masters see the error of their ways.

WRITE ABOUT A TIME WHEN YOU WERE DISOBEDIENT. WHAT WAS THE OUTCOME?

___

Nonconformity

RWE: "For nonconformity, the world whips you with its displeasure."

When you are different from the rest of the crowd, know that some people are **not** going to like it, and are going to figuratively whip you with their discontent. People don't like when you are dissimilar, and do you know why? Because they do not have the strength or courage to be unique as you. They are scared of your bravery, so instead of trying to understand you or respect you for following your own path, they will stop at nothing to tear you down. They would rather destroy you than put you up where you belong: ON A PEDESTAL! Your BEING YOU is something to absolutely be proud of, and if they cannot handle it, then that is entirely on them. Let them deal with their desire to whip you with their damn displeasure. You just keep being YOU in all of your unconventional, true-to-YOU ways!

IN WHAT WAYS ARE YOU A NONCONFORMIST?

___

HOW DOES BEING A NONCONFORMIST EMPOWER YOU?

___

HOW HAS BEING A NONCONFORMIST GOTTEN YOU INTO TROUBLE?

___

RWE: "Whoso who would be a man must be a nonconformist."

If you wish to be a "real man/woman," be a nonconformist. Ralph Waldo nailed it when he stated this truth. He knew back in the 1800's that you should not emulate everyone else. In this play of life, you were not born to act out a particular society-specified part. You were born to play YOU! If being you means **not** being like the rest of the crowd, then by all means DO YOU! Screw the masses! Are they who you want to follow anyways? Are they jumping for joy? Are they living up to their potential? I think not, or I wouldn't be writing this book. This book was written to help empower YOU- the one who needs that extra push of encouragement to get YOU done! So for cripes sake, Go for it! Design yourself in a unique fashion- literally and figuratively. You won't regret it!

IN WHAT WAYS CAN YOU DESIGN YOU EVEN BETTER THAN YOU ALREADY ARE?

_____
_____
_____
_____
_____
_____
_____

The Search

HDT: "Many men go fishing all of their lives without knowing that it is not fish they are after."

We do not all "fish" for the same things, and if we think we should, we are destined to live a miserable existence. We need to take time to really assess what it is we desire. Is it love? Money? A family? Creative freedom? Friendships? Health? Society seems to think it knows best what we want- a home, a family, and money, but it might not be what WE want. Please address this topic at your young age. Do not get sucked into a lifestyle of conformity. Are most of the adults you know happy? I do not know many who are. They are coping, managing, just getting by, and their dreams have since floated down the River of Regrets. I want more for you. You should want more for you too!

WHAT DO YOU WANT?

_____
_____
_____
_____
_____
_____

IF YOU GET WHAT YOU WANT, WHAT MIGHT YOUR LIFE LOOK LIKE? HOW WILL THAT MAKE YOU FEEL?

_____
_____
_____
_____
_____
_____

Self-Perspective

RWE: "A man is what he thinks about all day long."

What thoughts and feelings monopolize your mind? If your answers are negative ones, then we need to talk. If RWE is right, and "man is what he thinks about all day long," we need to pay particular attention to our thoughts and feelings as being mega-powerful forces! If you do not understand this at your young age, you may be designing a life of disaster for your future. You need to find a way to substitute your negative expectations with positive ones. You are a powerful being, and to continue thinking that life is a sour sack of shambles is going to ruin you emotionally, physically, spiritually, and financially! Please...I beg you to listen. THINK GOOD thoughts. Heck, think GREAT thoughts. Block out the bad! They are destiny damagers.

WHAT THOUGHTS CONSUME YOUR MIND DAILY?

_____
_____
_____
_____
_____
_____
_____

HOW ARE THESE THOUGHTS DESIGNING YOUR PRESENT LIFE? YOUR FUTURE?

_____
_____
_____
_____
_____
_____
_____

HOW MIGHT YOU ALTER THESE THOUGHTS TO PRODUCE A DIFFERENT OUTCOME?

_____
_____
_____
_____
_____
_____
_____

Gratitude

HDT: "I am grateful for what I am and have. My thanksgiving is perpetual."

Please do yourself and society a favor, and start being grateful. You *are* and you *have* so much. You are alive. Do you see the absolute gift of greatness in that? We must stop hourly (if we remember), and count our blessings. It must be an ongoing thanks. If we do this regularly, we invite more moments for which to be grateful. It is that easy! I am thankful for my career as a teacher. Every day, on the way to work, I thank "WHOMEVER" for allowing me to inspire young minds, and every day, I am given more opportunities to do so. For what are you grateful?

I AM GRATEFUL FOR:

_____
_____
_____
_____
_____
_____

Faith

"HDT: "We must walk consciously only part way toward our goal, and then leap in the dark to our success."

It is one thing to set goals, but we can make them come even faster into our existence when we believe they are possible- even when the odds seemed stacked against us. We need to take a leap of faith into the unknown. With this unwavering faith that it can be ours, we complete the cycle of faith. The faith that it exists and the faith that we deserve it. Only then can it become ours.

WHAT DO YOU BELIEVE IS ALREADY YOURS?

_____
_____
_____
_____
_____
_____

RWE: "All I have seen teaches me to trust the creator for all I have not seen."

We cannot explain a lot, and that right there should be evidence enough to realize that there must be a higher power at work who is crafting this game called life. She or He or You are orchestrating the band, and we are the musicians. What instrument do you strum, beat, or blow? How does it sound? Trust that you are here for a reason and that reason is to play a song of soulful sensation. You can contribute a melody of magnificence. Life will love you for it.

WHAT SONG WILL YOU PLAY?

_____
_____
_____
_____
_____
_____

Go Cray Cray

RWE: "I have lost my mental faculties, but am perfectly well."

Let's face it; we lose our minds now and again, but that is a good thing! Sometimes what is considered mentally sound is actually mentally insane! If what is "normal" is considered normal, then let me **not** be normal! Crazy is good. I am not talking about going out and acting like a raving lunatic, but I am talking about doing things differently. My 16 year old daughter and I sometimes go into Home Depot, and dance. We do not care what people think. We just sashay up and down the aisles- creating funky dance moves as we go along. Sometimes people will stop and stare, and other times they will laugh and smile, but we don't care. We just want to have fun, and as long as the crazy fun you create does no harm to you or others, why is it bad? It's not! That is why you should do it!

WHAT CRAZY THINGS HAVE YOU DONE LATELY, AND HOW DID THEY MAKE YOU FEEL?

_____
_____
_____
_____
_____
_____
_____

HDT: "Tis healthy to be sick sometimes."

How many of you have lost your marbles before? I mean, down and out, you went insane? It has happened to me hundreds of times throughout my life, and guess what? I am still here. People have seen me at my worst- especially when I was your age! I would cry, kick, scream, swear, punch walls, kick doors, and ya know what? It made me feel damn good to get it all out. Thoreau was right, "Tis healthy to be sick sometimes." It offers us a release of the negative energy that has built up in us for days, weeks, months, or possibly even years. Let it out. You'll be glad you did!

WHEN WAS THE LAST TIME YOU LOST YOUR MARBLES? WHAT HAPPENED? HOW WAS THAT HEALTHY FOR YOU?

_____
_____
_____
_____
_____
_____

Change

HDT: Things do not change; we change."

We always want to blame our lots in life on the situation having changed, but the reality is it is WE who have changed, and as a result of that, our *perception* of the situation has changed. We grow up, we are influenced by new ideas, newer people, we get hurt, we accumulate scars. These experiences shape the ways in which we view situations. We must stop accusing the circumstances so much as we should point a finger at our own interpretation of the circumstances, and how we chose to respond or react to it.

DISCUSS A TIME WHEN YOU CHANGED, BUT YOU BLAMED IT ON THE CIRCUMSTANCE:
_____
_____
_____
_____
_____
_____

Suffering

HDT: "The mass of men lead lives of quiet desperation.

Oh, how sad and confirming this is. I know so many people- older people who are living on isolated islands of sadness and distress, and they do so quietly. They dare not follow their dreams, be themselves, live in the now, and it is ruinous to their experiences here on Earth. Is **this** how we wish to live our lives? Does being alone do it for you? Do you aspire for greater desperation? If the answer is no, then you need to take the majority of advice offered in this book, and truly apply it. I want nothing more than to see you alter this quote into saying, "The mass of men lead lives of sonorous inspiration."

WHY DO YOU THINK PEOPLE ARE SO QUIETLY DESPERATE?
_____
_____
_____
_____
_____
_____

WHAT CAN WE DO TO HELP THEM OUT OF THIS RUT?
_____
_____
_____
_____
_____
_____

HDT: "Not until we are lost do we begin to understand ourselves."

There truly is no growth happening in our lives, unless we become lost. It is in the "getting lost" that we can become "found." Think about the times in your life when things were going swimmingly well. Did you learn much? Probably not. That is because the best gifts of learning often come wrapped in packages of despair and disappointment. From these persistently painful presents, we learn to re-adjust, re-claim, and re-design our life and our reactions to it. Isn't that special? So the next time life sends you a parcel of pain, embrace it, for it is in that moment, that you have the potential to grow exponentially!

WHEN WERE YOU "LOST," AND WHAT DID YOU "FIND?"

___
___
___
___
___
___

On Clothing

HDT: "Do not trouble yourself much to get new things, whether clothes or friends...Sell your clothes and keep your thoughts."

Our most precious commodities are our thoughts, but we do not understand this. We think it is our clothes or other material items of insignificance. When I think back to how much of my life I invested picking out "the right dress" or shoes, it seems ridiculous to me, for that was wasted time. I should have spent more of the clock reflecting about I was thinking. My thoughts are worth preserving. My clothes are not.

WHAT THOUGHTS OF YOURS ARE WORTH KEEPING? WHY?

___
___
___
___
___
___

HDT: "Distrust any enterprise that requires new clothes."

Basically, if a place makes you wear nice, new threads all of the time, it probably isn't a site where quality relationships are being built or fascinating ideas are being exchanged. Mostly it is a place where the value of humanity is being undermined, and that is probably not a place you want to work. EVER. This quote could apply to people you befriend and date as well. If someone is constantly trying to get you to change the way you dress yourself and others, you probably cannot trust them to be of any value to the development of your soul. An evolved being would not think the clothes make the man. She would think the man's mind makes the man.

HOW MANY TIMES HAS SOMEONE TRIED TO GET YOU TO CHANGE YOUR WAY OF DRESS? WHAT DID YOU DO? HOW DID IT FEEL?

___
___
___
___

HDT: "Every generation laughs at the old fashions, but follows religiously the new."

This one makes me laugh out loud, because it is so damn true. We look back and balk at garment styles of years' past, but yet we fall prey to the current trends, which will soon be laughable as well. We need to create our own sense of style. We are the creators of our true image. We do not need to be herded like sheep into clothing stores whose styles were created for the masses. We can generate our own sense of style through self-reflection. What styles do I like? What looks best on me? What colors suit me? What patterns fit my personality? What size feels comfortable to me? Which price tag fits my budget?

FASHION TRENDS I FOLLOWED AND PROBABLY SHOULD NOT HAVE:

_____
_____
_____
_____
_____

Music

HDT: "When I hear music, I fear no danger."

So many people would agree. Music soothes the soul in ways nothing else can. It can take us to a place of safety nothing else can. I always tell my children and students that I would be insane without music. It sustains me, it calms me, it invigorates and inspires me. When we are feeling lost or alone, all we have to do is put on an awesome piece of music, and all of our troubles can disintegrate into a sea of solace. When we feel angry or frustrated with our friends, family, or foes, we can escape by jamming out to something that really moves us. We are so lucky in that regard. We have to fear nothing when music plays. It is the great illustrator of life.

WHAT TYPES OF MUSIC DO YOU MOST ENJOY?

_____
_____
_____
_____
_____

HOW HAS MUSIC CHANGED YOUR LIFE?

_____
_____
_____
_____
_____

Lead By Example

HDT: "If you would convince a man that he does wrong, do right."

My students complain a lot about the world, and how negative it is, and I always tell them to get off their butts and lead the charge of change, by acting how they want to see others act. I want to see change in this world, so I decided to write this book. I know that it will lead to really fantastic movements of change around the globe. I could have just sat on my couch, watched negative news channels and cursed society for hours, but I elected to get out a computer and begin chronicling what it will take for people to really see that it is they who have the power to design changes they want to witness. If you want to see more goodness, be good. If you want to see more peace, be peaceful. If you want to see more productivity, be more productive. It isn't that hard to figure out. We lead by example. So, make your examples extraordinary!

WHAT "RIGHT" THINGS DO YOU CURRENTLY DO THAT COULD TEACH OTHERS?

_____
_____
_____
_____
_____
_____

Live

HDT: "I wanted to live deep and suck out all the marrow of life."

Most of us are surface creatures. We do not delve deep into life, and I believe that to be one of our biggest problems. We need to get inside the bone of life and extract all of its marrow-full meaning. We can no longer rest easily, by just knowing the minimal facts. We need to know the how's and the whys- not just the whos, whats, and whens. Once we can unravel a deeper meaning for it all, we can truly evolve into the beings of light we were predestined to become.

WHAT ARE YOUR DEEPEST THOUGHTS USUALLY ABOUT?

_____
_____
_____
_____
_____

WITH WHOM DO YOU SHARE THESE THOUGHTS AND WHY?

_____
_____
_____
_____

Let It Go

HDT: "It is only when we forget all of our learning that we begin to know."

Learning sounds like a good concept, but sometimes, it can be deemed bad. You see, when you learn something, it may not even be true. It might be something bad someone says about another or about you, and then you let it become a part of you and your knowledge base. Well, perhaps we'd be better off *not* knowing. In this regard, we could potentially abandon what we have learned, and start afresh. Perhaps in that moment or letting it "GO," we could resurface ourselves in the "KNOW."

WHAT MIGHT BE SOME GOOD THOUGHTS FOR YOU TO "UNLEARN?"

_____
_____
_____
_____
_____
_____

HDT: "A man is rich in proportion to the number of things he can afford to let alone."

Do you want to be emotionally wealthy? Well, I will tell you how; leave things alone. Let bygones be bygones. Let sleeping dogs lie. Forgive. Forget. People, if you could just master this one art, you could save yourself years of heartaches, headaches, and tears. We can become so rich by not holding on to past grudges, hates.

WHAT THINGS CAN YOU "LET ALONE?

_____
_____
_____
_____
_____

HOW MIGHT YOU BECOME ENLIGHTENED IF YOU DID FORGIVE AND FORGET?

_____
_____
_____
_____
_____

On Convincing Others

HDT: "Thaw with her gentle persuasion is more powerful than Thor with his hammer. The one melts, the other breaks into pieces."

Do not think you can effect great change in another or the masses with violent force. The only true way to get others to side with you is to melt things slowly with love. Think about times in your life when you felt emotionally moved by a movie or a moment. Chances are, it was a slow, powerful story of how love and obstacles can shape people. This touched you. It moved you, because it illustrated that love, although slower moving than a hammer of hate, has the potential to instill lessons about life that no violent object could ever hope to achieve. Now, think about a time when you tried to exert fury to get what you wanted. How did that work?

DISCUSS A TIME WHEN YOU ACTED LIKE <u>THOR</u> TO GET YOUR POINT ACROSS:
___
___
___
___
___
___
___

NOW, EXPLAIN A MOMENT WHEN YOU USED <u>THAW'S</u> APPROACH. WHAT WAS THE END RESULT?
___
___
___
___
___
___
___

You Are the Company You Keep

RWE: "As we are, so we associate."

Whoever we are is who we will most likely hang out with or date So if you are looking around at your current situation, and your cronies or significant others are acting obnoxious or rude, you might want to ask yourself how you, too, might be emulating this same type of behavior. We feel comfortable around similarities, and that is a scary notion if the people with whom we associate are troubled or trouble-causing individuals. People, please try to surround yourself with loving, supportive networks of people. You need to find those who care about you and humanity. If these individuals represent anything but goodness and truth, run for the hills!

WITH WHOM DO YOU ASSOCIATE, AND HOW IS THAT WORKING OUT FOR YOU?
___
___

RWE: "The good, by affinity, seek the good; the vile, by affinity, the vile."

LIKE attracts like. Have you ever noticed that generally good people tend to hang around generally good people, and all seem to be having a generally good time? And that bad people usually hang around with bad people and are usually are having a bad time? It makes sense, doesn't it? We attract who and what we are to ourselves. We also attract the circumstances which are attached to these people's behaviors. We need to become on high alert to these facts, so that we begin to pick and choose our acquaintances more carefully. You see, when we associate with these different types, we tend to bring their behaviors and outcomes of those behaviors into our own reality. For example, if I choose to befriend a group of gossipy girls, should I be surprised when they drive a figurative knife into my back the second I walk away? Or if choose kind-hearted companions, should I be surprised when I am in need of a shoulder to cry on that they are actually there for me? Should I be baffled when my party-going friends and I I receive Minor in Possession tickets for drinking at the beach? No. It is designed that way. "When you lie down with dogs, you are going to get fleas." Choose your friends wisely. Your future depends on it.

WHO HAS ATTRACTED TROUBLE TO YOUR LIFE?

WHO HAS ATTRACTED GOOD INTO YOUR LIFE?

HDT: "If misery loves company, misery has company enough."

There are enough nasty, negative people to populate an entire planet, and when they all find each other, may they all live unhappily ever after. Okay, that's mean, but I do know this; miserable people love miserable people, and when they get together, it is a Misery Fest. These individuals love to sit around and complain about every little slight they have experienced, are experiencing, or will experience in the future. Is it any wonder that they attract even more misery into their lives when they compound it with each other's stories? Oh, hell no! These people are destined to live on Anger Island for the rest of their lives, but you don't have to. You can go where the happy people inhabit- Gratitude Island- where life is abundant and fun!

WHICH ISLAND DO YOU CHOOSE? ANGER OR GRATITUDE? WHY?

_____
_____
_____
_____
_____

Materialism

RWE: "Great men are they who see that spiritual is stronger than any material force- that thoughts rule the world."

We are spiritual beings, and we need to recognize that our being so is more important than any other power. Too much emphasis is placed on money in today's society, and yet we are devoid of much happiness. We should be teaching today's kids to manage their spiritual bank accounts- not their monetary bank accounts. We need not worry about poverty of money as much as we should fret about poverty of spirit.

HOW ARE YOU A SPIRITUAL BEING?

_____
_____
_____
_____
_____
_____

WHAT DAMAGING EFFECTS HAS MATERIALISM HAD ON HUMANITY?

_____
_____
_____
_____
_____

HDT: "To have done anything just for money is to have been truly idle."

You cannot just accomplish things in life just for the cash. You have got to do things to for the betterment of humanity! To be idle is to move in no particular direction. This is what people do when their quest is for selfish reasons such as the mere acquisition of money. If we want to keep moving in our lives, we need to start finding a deeper reasoning for our working. It must be driven by more powerful forces such as love, compassion, desire for change. Only then are we moving forward and no longer idling.

HOW HAS PEOPLE'S QUEST FOR MONEY KEPT THEM IDLE?

_____
_____

LIST A FEW REASONS YOU WORK (OTHER THAN JUST FOR THE MONEY):

HDT: "That man is rich whose pleasures are the cheapest."

Oftentimes, we envy those who are rich, but the best things in life really are free- love, freedom, creativity, health. When we have these, we are we entirely wealthy.

WHAT ARE SOME PLEASURES YOU HAVE THAT ARE OF NO COST TO YOU??

Personal Gods

HDT: "Every people have gods to suit their circumstances."

We all look up to or pay homage to particular gods/goddesses/non-gods, etc., and that is PERFECTLY OKAY! We were designed with a built-in freedom to pick and choose who we *do* or *do not* worship. Why anyone cares what another believes is beyond me. I don't care if you want to worship your deviant dog as your savior! We need to stop shoveling our unwanted beliefs down other people's throats. Why can't we just be content believing what **we believe** behind closed doors? We aren't supposed to push people to worship as we do! All that does is create a resistance in people, which seizes them up, and makes them build walls of resistance.
If you truly want to see this world heal itself- start allowing people to freely regard their own personal gods. It is not for you to judge! Just consult your nearest theology "book." Ironically, almost all of them will agree.

WHEN HAS SOMEONE TRIED TO PUSH THEIR BELIEFS ON YOU? HOW DID YOU LIKE IT AND WHAT DID YOU DO?

Life

RWE: "It is not the length of life, but depth of life."

It is not the years of life that matter, but what is done in those years that is most important. Oftentimes, I will hear my students say that they want to live until they are at least ninety. What I do not hear them say is what they intend to do in those ninety years that will change this world. They talk nothing of the contributions they wish to make. They talk nothing of the happiness they intend to create. They simply think life is a duration- not a game-changing station. People, we are here to live deeply, feel deeply, love deeply! Length of life isn't a number- it is an experience!

WHAT PLANS DO YOU HAVE FOR YOUR LIFE? WHERE DO YOU WANT TO GO? WHAT DO YOU WANT TO DO? HOW CAN YOU EFFECT GREAT CHANGE?

_____
_____
_____
_____
_____
_____

HDT: "How could youths better learn to live than by at once trying the experiment of living."

You young people need to give life a chance. After all, it is the only way you will see it for the preciousness it contains. Get out in nature, swing from a rope and jump into the water, ride a bike through your neighborhood, dance until you are drenched in salty sweat beads, ask out that person you think is attractive and intelligent, or write that magnificent story. For crying out loud, stop watching life unrealistically unfold on a television or computer screen. You are wasting this present called life! It is meant to be cherished, understood, and loved. I hear so many kids complaining about how much life sucks, but they contribute nothing to experience it, so that is what life gives them- NOTHING! You get what you expect. If you say, "Life's a bitch, and then you die," you are RIGHT! Quit cursing life, and start cursing yourself for being a wimp who is NOT trying life on for size! You only have yourself to blame!

THINGS I WASTE MY "LIFE" TIME DOING:

_____
_____
_____
_____
_____
_____

THINGS I SHOULD BE DOING WITH MY "LIFE" TIME:

_____

_____
_____
_____
_____
_____

Bad/Mean People Suck

HDT: "It is best to avoid the beginnings of evil."

Stay away from psychopathic people. Believe me, they are out there. Usually when you first meet others, you can size them up by the vibes you get, while in their presence. If you get a bad feeling, it is usually right. If a person makes your stomach ill from the negative words that come out of his/her mouth or the actions they display, you may want to take notice, and hightail it outta there. AS QUICKLY AS POSSIBLE. In my 46 years on this planet, I have learned that some people are just plain poisonous to be around, and it is better that I exit their presence fast. I cannot afford to allow their negative energy to infiltrate my being. You need to be aware of this. These could be potential friends, dates, employers, or even strangers. Trust me, if they make you sick, they are probably sick. Move away. Let the vile attract the vile. You go out and meet you some positive peeps! :)

DISCUSS A TIME IN TIME IN YOUR LIFE WHEN YOU GOT A BAD VIBE ABOUT SOMEONE. WERE YOU RIGHT? HOW?

_____
_____
_____
_____
_____
_____

HDT: "The savage man is never quite eradicated."

There will always be bad people in this world. That is a fact. The question becomes, what can YOU do to make sure you are not one of them? How hard have you been working being a great BEING? One person I know very well talks nonstop about how much he hates this world, because it is full of "bad" people. He elects to see only the negative. It has consumed this person so much, that he often speaks of killing himself to escape. It makes me so sad that he cannot see any good in people, when in reality, there are far more good people than there are bad. People, what you focus on, you bring into your reality. This all comes down to how you handle the savages. Do you befriend them? Date them? Are they your parents? Are they your teachers? Are the strangers? Politicians? How are YOU allowing them to infiltrate your mind? Impede your success? Why would you CHOOSE to give them this power? Let it go. There will always be jerky people in this world, and as long as you keep giving all of your attention and hatred towards them, you will continue to let these beasts live rent-free in your mind! STOP!

<u>HERE IS A LIST OF SAVAGES THAT I AM GOING TO RELEASE FROM THE CONFINES OF MY MIND AND ATTENTION:</u>

IF I LET THESE BEASTS OF BURDEN GO, THE FOLLOWING MIGHT HAPPEN:

A Job Well Done

HDT: What is once well-done is done forever."

Do it well, and you will never have to do it again. I see so many kids have to repeat classes in my high school, because the first time they tried, they really didn't try at all. Just think, if they had just done the job right the first time, they would not have to take the time to do it all over again. Life is kind of like that too. If we just complete tasks in a timely manner, we can move forward and learn and experience more, but if we do a half-assed job, then we keep having to repeat the same menial work over and over again until it is done right. In this regard, we just create more and more work for ourselves. Why are we so reluctant to do it right in the first place? I don't know. Perhaps we really are addicted to pain.

WHAT HAVE YOU DONE REALLY WELL, THAT YOU'LL NEVER HAVE TO DO AGAIN?

IN WHAT AREAS OF YOUR LIFE HAVE YOU LEFT THINGS POORLY MADE, AND WILL HAVE TO SOMEHOW RE-DO?

Being Alone Is Company Enough

HDT: "I love to be alone. I never found the companion that was so companionable as solitude."

I have so many students who think if they just find the right girlfriend or boyfriend, their life will magically complete itself. Ha! Ha! What a laugh! Weeks later they are in my classroom crying about how "they got screwed over." "No, honey," I say, "You screwed yourself over when you took stock in another's power without first investing in yourself. You are your own greatest commodity! See the value in you, believe it, achieve it, and receive it, and perhaps you'll not be sobbing on your teacher's shoulder anymore.

ALONE, HOW ARE YOU GREAT FOR YOU?

_____
_____
_____
_____
_____
_____

HDT: "I have a great deal of company in the house, especially in the morning when nobody calls."

When we are left alone, without interruption, we can really be an absolute joy to be with. How much can you stand to be alone? Do you love it? If so, create more opportunities to be solitary. During this time as a lone wolf, you can get a lot accomplished, have the peace to meditate, and work on the pursuits which are of greatest interest to you. This is such a healthy thing to do for YOU, so by all means, go for it!

IF YOU HAD AN ENTIRE WEEK (WITHOUT INTERRUPTION) TO YOURSELF, WHAT WOULD YOU DO?

_____
_____
_____
_____
_____
_____

Karma

RWE: "There is a tendency for things to right themselves."

Things will fix themselves whether we want them to or not. Whether you wish to believe it or not, we get what is coming to us. This means if you are constantly being good to the world, the world will be good back to you. Conversely, if you are a mean to the world, don't be shocked when it is mean back.

HAVE YOU EVER WITNESSED A "KARMIC" EVENT? WHAT WAS THE NATURE OF THE SITUATION? GOOD OR BAD, DID THAT PERSON HAVE IT COMING TO THEM?

___
___
___
___
___
___

RWE: "What you are comes to you."

This is a hard pill to swallow. "You mean if I am an absolute jackass to people, I will get treated like one myself?" Yep! It may take a while, but the laws of your actions will catch up to you. I have witnessed numerous bosses of mine who treated their employees like garbage who, down the road, ultimately got fired in the worst ways. Did they deserve it? You betcha! They were mean, spiteful, and looking for everyone's flaws. Eventually, all of their meanness was examined too, and they ended up losing their jobs- just as they had removed so many others'. Just think if they had been kind. Where might they be today? Perhaps gainfully employed.

HAVE YOU EVER HAD SOMETHING BAD HAPPEN TO YOU THAT YOU DESERVED? WHAT WAS IT? HOW DID YOU HANDLE IT?

___
___
___
___
___
___

Let Others Shine

RWE: "A great man is always willing to be little."

It is good when we let other people receive credit. We do not always need to the star of the show. It is important that we let other people shine as well. When we do this, we open up a confidence in them that really helps catapult their psyches into well-being. Just think; if we all allowed others to be recognized for their great feats instead of trying to outdo them, we could make great changes on this planet. People's confidences would rise and overall, the amount of happiness and productivity would increase.

WRITE ABOUT A PERSON WHOM YOU SHOULD LET SHINE:

___
___
___
___
___

WHAT MIGHT HAPPEN TO HIM/HER AS A RESULT OF YOUR ALLOWING IT?

_____
_____
_____
_____
_____
_____
_____

Time

RWE: "The years teach much which the days never know."

Each day is not capable of teaching us what years can. Life has been relegated to 365 calendar days per year. That sounds like a lot of days, but each 24 hour period is not that momentous in its ability to teach us a whole heck of a lot. Life is more of a perspective piece, which when measured by years, has the potential to illustrate more to us as human beings than we can even fathom. When we try to recapture the essence of our pasts, we usually do so by remembering large chunks of time. A lot of you young people will remember things by grade. For instance, you might say, "I remember in 6th grade, I learned of my parents' divorce, and how much that screwed me up." That year was wrought with your witnessing arguments, fear, uncertainty, and depression. In this case, you learned a lot *that* particular year! Years are a powerful force from which to ascertain A LOT of life's lessons. Reflecting back on your childhood, which years stand out most and why?

THE YEARS I LEARNED A LOT & WHY?

_____
_____
_____
_____
_____
_____
_____

Get It On Your Own

HDT: "It is the greatest of all advantages to enjoy no advantage at all."

You need to have NO leg up on the competition. It will not do you as much good as you think. Some people are born lucky. They may have been given a spectacular talent from birth, they may have been blessed with wealthy parents, or they may just have won on an instant lottery ticket. The reality is, you are better off NOT having those advantages from the start. True growth comes from the struggle. Think about times in your life when things were going really well for you. How did you develop from that? I am betting not a lot! Now, think of obstacles you have faced throughout your time here. What did they teach you? I am betting a ton! We experience the most growth when we are NOT given advantages, because it makes us work harder and appreciate the outcomes more. Disadvantages are an opportunity to see a problem, seek a solution, and feel empowered when we solve it. What are some obstacles you have faced, and what did they teach you?

OBSTACLES I FACED AND WHAT THEY TAUGHT ME:

_____
_____
_____
_____
_____
_____

HDT: "The man who goes alone can start today, but he who travels with another must wait till that other is ready."

Do not wait for other people to be ready to seek what it is you desire. The truth is, they may NEVER be ready. We cannot rely on and wait for other people to go after our dreams at the same time as us. We are separate souls- on differing paths. We must follow our intentions NOW- without hesitation. Let other people go when they are ready. Our time begins now.

WHOM HAVE YOU ALLOWED TO HOLD YOU BACK FROM STARTING YOUR LIFE?

_____
_____
_____
_____
_____
_____

WHAT MIGHT YOU BE ABLE TO ACCOMPLISH IF YOU LEAVE WITHOUT THEM?

_____
_____
_____
_____
_____
_____

RWE: "Every artist was at first an amateur."

These quotes tell us that we all have to start somewhere. We are not born great. We have to work at it! Some people do have great talents bestowed upon them, but for the most part, those who met with tremendous success did so with practice and courage. What skills would you like to develop? How might you go about pursuing them?

SKILLS & TALENTS I'D LIKE TO DEVELOP ON MY OWN & WAYS I CAN:

_____
_____
_____
_____
_____
_____

The Impression That I Get

RWE: "The best effort of a fine person is felt after we have left their presence."

We do not always understand the value of another until they have left us. Sometimes a friendship dissolves, a family separates, a person moves away, or, in the worst case scenario, that person dies. Who has left your presence, and you felt it? What did their absence do to you personally?

THE PERSON WHO LEFT AND HOW IT IMPACTED ME:

_____
_____
_____
_____
_____
_____

Being Busy

HDT: "It is not enough to be busy. So are the ants. The question is: What are we busy about?"

Ants work hard staying busy. They seek food, shelter, and mates. Their being busy serves a genuine purpose. You are busy too, but is what you occupy your time with a worthwhile endeavor? How much time do you spend on Snapchat, Instagram, Facebook, watching television, playing video games, and sleeping? Where should we spend our time busying ourselves? If today were our last day on Earth, would we be proud to know we spent it perusing ridiculous posts made by others, or by killing the character on the computer screen? If you could replace the time you are "busy" doing these things, for what might you exchange it?

I WOULD EXCHANGE MY "BUSY" TIME
DOING_____

WITH MY MORE VALUABLE TIME
DOING_____

From Within

HDT: "What lies behind us and what lies ahead of us are tiny matters compared to what lies within us."

Better than anyone else, we know the true essence of who we are. Why can we not trust this? We spend so much time entrenched in drudging up the past or fantasizing about our futures, that we forget to remember that what is currently inside of us is all that matters. You cannot rewind the NOW, and change any of it. You cannot fast forward the PRESENT, and expect to know its outcome. All you can do is tap into the gift of self-knowledge, listen to it, honor it, and act upon it. Only then will you know its magnificence. My students come to class each day and talk and write incessantly about their childhoods. Mostly this entails their telling of divorce, dysfunctional parents, drug and alcohol abuse, and struggles with poverty. They cannot let go of these human hurts. They love to constantly bring up the pain that permeates. In this way, they are hanging on to their hurtful histories. They cannot see the ways in which this reminiscing holds them hostage, and keeps them in a permanent state of non-growth. They need to let go of the past, and focus on what currently resides in themselves, which is of much greater significance. It is what is within you that will guide YOU. Nothing outside of you completes you. Nothing!

WHAT LIES WITHIN YOU?

_____
_____
_____
_____
_____
_____
_____

Conclusion

Writing this book has really helped me. How has it helped you? In what ways did you use it? In what other ways can you see it being used?

I would like to offer you the opportunity to take one last moment to reflect on this book's contents and what they meant to you personally.

WHAT HAVE YOU LEARNED_____

ABOUT LIFE?
ABOUT YOURSELF?
ABOUT OTHERS?
ABOUT SCHOOL?
ABOUT WORK?
ABOUT LOVE?
ABOUT HATE?
ABOUT ATTITUDE?
ANYTHING?

Please feel free to fill in as much of the spaces below, and then take a picture of your writing with your phone and send it to my e-mail address- riddyengle@hotmail.com. Call it

_____'s Conclusion

(insert your first and last name here).

The contents of your answer/s may be used for a future book I am writing. With your submission, comes your desire to possibly be a part of that work. Additionally, you may be selected to participate in a future filmed-documentary about Transcendental Teens.

Thank you so much for taking the time to read and apply these Transcendental emotional enlightenment tools. It is my hope that you will now go out and CHANGE the WORLD the way you wish to see it.

RWE: "Some books leave us free and some books make us free."

If this book helped you in any way, I need you to tweet about it- NOW!! Tell people how good it was! Tell people what it did for you!

Get with friends, and discuss answers.

ALSO, LET "THE TRANSCENDENTAL TEEN" COME TO YOUR SCHOOL!

CONTACT US AT: motivatingmindslifecoaching.com

for a chance to participate in a workshop that could show your classmates and you just how YOU ALL can change the world!

Email us at: info@motivatingminds.com

Our transcendental journey has come to an end. Take these tools and use them with you the rest of your lives. I promise they will bring you HAPPINESS!!!!!!!

Thanks, RWE & HDT, for YOUR FABULOUS inspiration! We will change the world with your ideas!

Sincerely,

Christy Engle

Motivating Minds Community